A-Z of Scots Education Law – a guide for parents (Third Edition)

Text written by

Sandra McGuire and Iain Nisbet

Edited by

Jennifer Wallace

Senior Policy Advocate

Consumer Focus Scotland

Fòcas Luchd-Caitheimh Alba
Comhairle Luchd-caitheimh ùr na h-Alba

Consumer Focus Scotland
Scotland's new Consumer Council

⊠ TSO
information & publishing solutions

First published 2001

ISBN 978 0114973469

Contents

Preface

This is the third edition of the highly popular reference book on Scots education law. The first two editions were published by one of our predecessor organisations, the Scottish Consumer Council. Since the previous edition in 2004 there have been a number of major changes, in particular the Scottish Schools (Parental Involvement) Act 2006, which are updated in this version.

This A-Z offers parents an easy to use reference to the law on all aspects of children's education in Scotland. Young people may also be interested in the book, as their rights are also covered throughout. We also think that the A-Z will be of interest to teachers, education officials, teacher educators and anybody else whose work brings them in touch with parents, young people and children. It will arm parents and their advisers with the information they need to get the best out of the education system. It covers the key pieces of legislation, including the Education (Scotland) Act 1981, the Standards in Scotland's Schools etc Act 2000 and the Education (Additional Support for Learning) Act 2004. It also covers other areas of the law relating to education hidden away in other statutes, that parents may be less aware of but which may still be important to them. In addition there are a number of "grey areas" of education about which the law has relatively little to say, such as what should be taught at school and which are included in this A-Z.

The first edition was prepared by Sandra McGuire and Iain Nisbet, while Iain carried out the updating for the second and third editions – Consumer Focus Scotland is indebted to them both. Although the A-Z should not be regarded as an authoritative statement of the law, which only the courts can determine we believe it will be a valuable source of reference for all Scots in their contact with the education system.

Douglas Sinclair
Chair, Consumer Focus Scotland

About Consumer Focus Scotland

Consumer Focus Scotland started work in October 2008. Consumer Focus Scotland was formed through the merger of three organisations – the Scottish Consumer Council, energywatch Scotland, and Postwatch Scotland.

Consumer Focus Scotland works to secure a fair deal for consumers in both private markets and public services, by promoting fairer markets, greater value for money, and improved customer service. While producers of goods and services are usually well-organised and articulate when protecting their own interests, individual consumers very often are not. The people whose interests we represent are consumers of all kinds: they may be patients, tenants, parents, solicitors' clients, public transport users, or shoppers in a supermarket.

We have a commitment to work on behalf of vulnerable consumers, particularly in the energy and post sectors, and a duty to work on issues of sustainable development.

www.consumerfocus-scotland.org.uk

Acknowledgements

Previous editions of this A-Z were published by the Scottish Consumer Council, now Consumer Focus Scotland. We remain indebted to Sandra McGuire and Iain Nisbet of the Govan Law Centre, who drafted the text for the first edition of this book and Iain Nisbet who carried out the updating for both the second edition and this edition. We are deeply grateful to the many people and organisations who took the time to meet with the Scottish Consumer Council to discuss the progress of the first edition book and who commented on the draft text, of both the first and second editions, often at short notice.

In particular our thanks go to:

Eilish Garland, Edinburgh Advice and Conciliation Service

Judith Gillespie, Scottish Parent Teacher Council

Shelley Gray, Children in Scotland

Ann Hill, Scottish School Board Association

David Leadbetter, CALM Training Limited

Alastair Macbeth

Katy Macfarlane, Scottish Child Law Centre

Maurice Plaskow, UK Education Forum

Alison Preuss, Schoolhouse Home Education Association

Sue Ross, Tourette Scotland

Kay Stairs, Glasgow City Council

Kay Tisdall, University of Edinburgh

CoSLA

The Scottish Government

The Housing, Education and Local Government Committee of the Scottish Consumer Council oversaw the production of the first edition of this book. Its members were:

Ann Clark (committee chair)

Jenny Hamilton

John Hanlon

Alex Wright

Martyn Evans (ex-officio)

Graeme Millar (ex-officio)

The administrative support for the production of this third edition was provided by Louis Cowan of Consumer Focus Scotland.

Introduction

What is this A-Z for?

This is an A-Z guide for parents to the law in Scotland about children's education. It will help you to understand and deal with the sorts of decisions, difficulties or problems you may be faced with in your child's education. You should find answers in this A-Z to a lot of the questions you are likely to ask about your legal responsibilities and rights in education. Not every single problem or difficulty that may arise can of course be covered, mainly because there are no clear-cut answers to many of the questions parents ask. Certain issues, like the safety and supervision of pupils, have not been clearly resolved in a legal sense, and where this is the case, we say so.

The A-Z attempts to:

- tell you about your legal responsibilities and rights over a wide range of matters to do with your child's education. It also says what education authorities and schools must do and what they needn't do in connection with that;

- indicate what sorts of services and arrangements you can expect to be provided for your child's education over and above what the law requires. A lot of these services and provisions (such as how children are taught at school) are not laid down by law at all, but result from the policies and practices of education authorities or schools;

- point to steps you could take on your own or with others to make sure that your legal responsibilities and rights are properly respected, and what to do if they are not. Bear in mind, though, that a lot of matters to do with your child's education are not legally enforceable. Rather, they will depend on the amount of co-operation or goodwill between education authorities, teachers, parents and pupils.

What's in this A-Z?

The book begins with an explanation of children's rights, and your basic responsibilities and rights as a parent. It then deals with a whole range of topics, presented in alphabetical order. Questions dealt with include:

- Can you be forced to send your child to school?
- Do you have any choice of school?
- Do you have any educational rights if your child is looked after by the local authority?
- What legal rights do school pupils have?
- Must certain things be taught at school?
- Can your child be made to wear school uniform?
- What punishment can schools give to your child?
- Are schools allowed to charge you for anything?
- Can you insist on homework being given?
- What sort of information about schools are you entitled to?
- How much responsibility do schools have for your child's safety?
- Is there anything education authorities must do before they are allowed to close down a school?
- What can happen if the school rules are disobeyed?
- What is your legal position when teachers go on strike?

And many more! Special sections cover getting advice and help, making a complaint and taking legal action. The role and duties of official bodies like the Scottish Government and education authorities are also covered. Other sections deal with things like the employment of schoolchildren, school inspections, discrimination, human rights, and additional support needs. For further information about these and other topics, you are referred to various other publications and useful web sites as well. A good background introduction to the Scottish education system can be found in the Parent Zone web site at: http://www.ltscotland.org.uk/parentzone/.

Topics are arranged alphabetically. If the section you are looking at does not answer your question fully, you may find it is dealt with under other sections. Check the "*see also*" suggestions at the end of each section for cross-references.

Sometimes it is useful to be able to find the relevant legislation. References to these are given at the end of most sections. You should be able to get copies of them through The Stationery Office and in most central reference libraries. A useful web site is http://www.opsi.gov.uk/legislation/, where you will be able to access all legislation since 1988 about education, and updated or revised legislation from before then.

A lot of law is found in regulations (or "statutory instruments") instead of an Act. Again, these are referred to at the end of many sections. You should be able to get copies of regulations through The Stationery Office or central reference libraries. Again, www.opsi.gov.uk/legislation/ will give you internet access to regulations since 1987.

The government also gives guidance, normally called "circulars", to bodies such as education authorities in carrying out various laws, although they cover a lot of non-legal matters as well. Most do not carry the force of law, advising or recommending what should be done, not what must be done. Some circulars, however, contain statutory guidance which does carry the force of law. Circulars themselves should make clear whether they do or not. Circulars are important in giving you an indication about how the government expects particular laws or policies to be put into practice. Relevant ones are, again, given at the end of sections. You can get copies of circulars from the Scottish Government.

On some occasions the Scottish Government or UK Government arranges for statutory Codes of Practice to be published rather than guidance. Codes of Practice generally outline minimum standards of service. For example, the Disability Rights Commission published the statutory Code of Practice for disability discrimination in schools and a Code of Practice for Additional Support for Learning was published by the Scottish Government.

Sometimes the law can be ambiguous and difficult to interpret. In such cases, it can be useful to see what decisions have been made by the courts (if any). Significant court cases are highlighted throughout the book.

You may wish to find more information about a particular topic, and many sections in this book give you a list of other publications or web sites that can tell you more. Contact details for all of the organisations mentioned in the book are given at the end.

This A-Z should not be regarded as the "last word" in the law – this rests with the courts. You will find a special section about where to go for further advice and help. Every effort has been made, at the time of going to press, to bring this A-Z up to date with the latest or impending changes in the law, but readers should consult a solicitor or other legal adviser about any further changes in the law since the date of publication.

Overview – Children's Rights

Human Rights

The basic rights of all human beings, including children, can be found in the European Convention for the Protection of Human Rights and Fundamental Freedoms, signed by the UK in 1950. These rights were included in UK law through the Human Rights Act 1998, and include the right to respect for family and private life and the right to education. More detail on these can be found in the **Human Rights** section of this book.

The United Nations Convention on the Rights of the Child (1989)

The UK ratified this Convention in 1991. The Convention sets out the basic legal rights which should be enjoyed by every child.

These include:

- all rights under the Convention must be available to all children without discrimination of any kind;
- the best interests of the child must be a primary consideration in all actions concerning the child;
- the child's views must be considered and taken into account in all matters affecting the child, subject to the child's age and maturity.

Other articles can be divided into three areas: participation (e.g. right to information); provision (e.g. health or education services); and protection (e.g. an adequate standard of living, protection from abuse).

By ratifying the Convention, countries agree to use these basic rights as their minimum standard, and to introduce legislation to remedy gaps in the protection they offer children. Countries have to provide reports on what steps they have taken to comply with the requirements of the Convention. It is not possible however to rely on UN Convention rights in Scottish courts nor to bring a case against the Scottish or Westminster Parliaments for failing to introduce legislation. Scotland's Commissioner for Children and Young People is able to carry out formal investigations of services – including schools – in relation to children's rights (see **Scotland's Commissioner for Children and Young People** for further information).

The UK has taken steps to comply with the Convention. Probably the most important piece of Scottish legislation relating to children since it signed the Convention has been the Children (Scotland) Act 1995. This goes further than any other Act in establishing children as individuals with rights (and responsibilities) of their own, but also reinforces the need for children to have additional protection. In education law specifically, the Standards in Scotland's Schools etc. Act 2000 introduced a number of important concepts from the Convention into Scots law.

Domestic Law

In many areas of the law (e.g. the law relating to damages and compensation) children have the same rights as adults. So long as they have a sufficient level of understanding, children can consult a solicitor and (if necessary) raise a court action in their own name. Some laws give rights only to a specific group of people, such as parents.

Sometimes, domestic legislation gives rights to children, which were previously only enjoyed by adults. An example of this in education is the child's right to appeal against an exclusion from school.

Many parental rights are only exercisable to promote the child's well-being. A parent's decision or action could be challenged, when exercising such a parental right. The challenge could be made because it is not in the child's best interests or it goes against the child's views.

Conversely, some rights of the child are subject to parental limitations. Every child of school age has the right to school education, provided by the education authority. However, this doesn't affect the parents' discretion on how they wish to educate their child. So, for example, parents can insist on their child attending an independent school, even where the child would rather attend an education authority school.

Children now also have rights to have their views taken into account by the education authority when it takes decisions that significantly affect them. This only applies where the child has a wish to express their views and so there is no express duty to solicit those views. The weight that will be given to a child's views and opinions will vary depending on the age and maturity of the child.

See also

Consulting children
Human Rights
Scotland's Commissioner for Children and Young People

Useful organisations

Article 12 in Scotland
Children in Scotland
Scotland's Commissioner for Children and Young People

Useful publications

Scottish Alliance for Children's Rights (2008) *The NGO Alternative Report (Scotland) to the United Nations Committee on the Rights of the Child* published by SACR

Cleland, A. and Sutherland, E. (2001) *Children's Rights in Scotland* 2nd edition published by W. Greens.

Hodgkin, R. and Newell, P. (2002) *Implementation Handbook for the Convention on the Rights of the Child* Revised edition available from UNICEF

United Nations (1989) *The Convention on the Rights of the Child* General Assembly of the United Nations

Legal references used in this section

UN Convention on the Rights of the Child

Section 30(2); Education (Scotland) Act 1980

Children (Scotland) Act 1995

Section 1; Standards in Scotland's Schools etc. Act 2000

Overview –
Parents' Responsibilities and Rights

For the purposes of education law the term "parent" includes:

• a guardian;

• anyone who has parental responsibility for a child;

• anyone who has a duty to pay maintenance for a child; or

• anyone who has day to day care and control of a child.

What are parents' basic responsibilities?

Parents are legally responsible for making sure that their children are properly educated once they reach school age (approx. 5 years old). This is normally by making sure that their children regularly attend a school which is managed by the education authority. It is possible for a child to be educated at home, at an independent school, or somewhere else instead. The law does not say exactly what sort of education should be provided. It uses the words "efficient education" without saying what this means, except that it should be suitable to a child's age, ability and aptitude.

Parental responsibilities continue until a child reaches school leaving age (approx. 16 years old). On reaching school leaving age young people normally become responsible for their own education – unless a mental illness, developmental disorder, learning disability or inability to communicate means they are unable to do so. However, parents may be expected to contribute financially if a young person decides to carry on at school or college after they are 16 years old. Grants, bursaries or other financial assistance may be available (see **Fees and charges** and **Financial assistance**).

Parents have a number of special legal duties in connection with their children's education. These duties include:

- making sure their children are properly educated, either by regular attendance at school or "by other means", for example by attendance at an independent school or by home education (see **Home education**, **Flexi-schooling**, **Attendance and absence** and **Independent schools**);
- seeing that their children obey school rules (see **School rules**);
- making sure that their children attend school adequately and suitably dressed, so they can take advantage of the schooling offered (see **Clothing and uniform**);
- making proper arrangements for their children's safety and supervision outside school hours (e.g. while walking to school).

The basic rights of parents

Parents have the right to influence the education their children receive, within limits. The education authority has to "have regard" to the general principle that children should be educated in accordance with their parents' wishes. However, this must be compatible with efficient and suitable instruction and must avoid unreasonable public expenditure. Parents' wishes are only one of a number of factors that the education authority must consider in taking decisions.

It is a principle of European Human Rights law that children are to be educated in accordance with the religious and philosophical convictions of their parents. This is subject to the same limitations as in domestic law (see **Human Rights**).

Parents also have the right to choose which school their children attend (see **Choice of school**), although there are certain limited circumstances where the first choice of school will not be available.

Do parents have other rights?

Parents also have a number of more specific rights. Parents have rights to:

- receive certain written information about schools and education within their area (see **Information for parents**);
- be consulted about school closures and other similar changes (see **Consulting parents** and **School closures and changes**);
- have their children educated without having to pay fees, although charges may be payable for certain items and some additional specialist tuition (see **Fees and charges**);
- be consulted about and appeal against decisions made about their children's additional support needs) (see **Additional Support for Learning**);
- appeal against an exclusion of their child from school (see **Exclusion from school**);
- withdraw their children from religious education and observance (and from sex education classes) (see **Religious education and observance** and **Sex education**);
- have their children taught in Gaelic (see **Gaelic**); and
- in certain circumstances, receive assistance with clothing, boarding accommodation, meals and milk, transport, grants and other financial assistance (see **Financial assistance**, **Clothing and uniform**, and **Food and Drink**).

Where parents have problems about services which must be provided by law, it is advisable to discuss them with school staff first. If this is not satisfactory, complaints may be made to the education authority, or even to the Scottish Ministers (see **Complaints**).

The rest of this book provides detailed information on all of the above-mentioned responsibilities and rights of parents.

See also

Consulting parents
Information for parents
Parental involvement and representation

Useful organisations

Parentzone

Useful publications

Scottish Executive (2006) *Parents as Partners in their Children's Learning: Toolkit* (available from the Scottish Government)

Legal references used in this section

Section 1(3) of the Children (Scotland) Act 1995

Sections 1, 3, 9, 22, 22A, 22D, 28A, 28H, 28I, 28J, 28K, 30, 31,32, 33, 54, 57, 61 of the Education (Scotland) Act 1980

Reg 4A of the Schools General (Scotland) Regulations 1975

Sections 5 and 6 of the Standards in Scotland's Schools etc. (Scotland) Act 2000

Circular no. 2/2001 "Standards in Scotland's Schools etc. Act 2000: Conduct of Sex Education in Scottish Schools."

Wyatt v. Wilson 1994SLT 1135

ACCESSIBILITY STRATEGIES

Every education authority, independent school and grant-aided school must have an accessibility strategy.

An accessibility strategy is a strategy, over a three year period, for:

• improving access to the curriculum for disabled pupils;

• improving physical access for disabled pupils; and

• improving access to information normally provided in writing for disabled pupils.

Accessibility strategies should also cover pre-school education and the education of traveller children.

Access to the curriculum

An accessibility strategy must set down the ways in which the authority or school will increase the extent to which disabled pupils can participate in the curriculum.

Disabled pupils should be able to access a full and broad curriculum, similar to that followed by other pupils, as far as possible. Disabled pupils may also need additional support or different approaches to teaching to help them to learn and benefit from the curriculum. Accessibility strategies should take a strategic approach to removing barriers to learning.

Scottish Goverment guidance suggests that authorities or schools should consider the following when drawing up an accessibility strategy:

• distribution of learning support and auxiliary provision across the authority's schools;

• provision of auxiliary aids for pupils with certain disabilities;

- staff training;
- alternative approaches for teaching and support;
- sharing good practice;
- collaboration with other schools and agencies;
- integration of approach for pupils with combined educational /health/social needs;
- overcoming barriers to extra-curricular activities;
- accessibility of information and communications technology, including;
- consideration of pupils with different types of disability.

Physical access to schools

An accessibility strategy must set out the authority's or school's strategic plans to improve the physical environment, with a view to increasing the extent to which disabled pupils are able to take advantage of the education and associated services provided there.

An education authority's accessibility strategy should include plans for improvements to enable disabled children to attend, wherever possible, the school of their choice and to access all areas and activities of that school.

The guidance has a list of improvements which may be required, listed below.

Physical access

- Ramps
- Handrails
- Widened doorways
- Lifts
- Automatic doors
- Accessible toilets, showers and changing areas
- Adapted furniture and equipment
- Sufficient floor space for manoeuvring wheelchairs
- Floor coverings
- Evacuation procedures

Access for those with visual impairments

• Improved signage
• Route finding systems
• Colour contrasting
• Adjustable lighting
• Tactile paving
• Evacuation procedures

Access for those with hearing impairments

• Induction loops
• Radio systems
• Infra-red systems
• Light signals
• Sound insulation
• Floor coverings
• Evacuation procedures

Access for those with other disabilities

• Additional space requirements
• Pupil support bases
• Quiet rooms
• Sensory rooms
• Therapy rooms

Access to information

An accessibility strategy must set out the authority's or school's strategic plans to improve communication with disabled pupils. In particular, the authority or school should seek to provide information normally provided to pupils in writing in alternative formats. The information should be provided in a format that takes into account the preferences of the pupil and/or the pupil's parent(s), and should be provided within a reasonable time.

"Alternative formats" might include information provided:

- orally;
- on audio tape;
- by sign language interpreter;
- by lip speaking;
- on video tape (with sign language / subtitles);
- in Braille;
- in large print;
- in an "easy read" format;
- on CD-Rom;
- by other accessible electronic communication.

This means that the following should be available in alternative formats (though this list is not exhaustive):

- class handouts and worksheets;
- textbooks;
- timetables;
- school handbooks;
- test and examination papers;
- posters used in school;
- information about school events.

The authority or school will also require to plan carefully in advance so that information in alternative formats can be provided within a reasonable time. In many cases (e.g. test papers) the alternative format will be required at the same time as the written information.

Education Authority Planning

Education authorities may incorporate their accessibility strategies into their improvement plans or annual statements of improvement objectives. If the authority does this, then the school should have regard to the accessibility strategy when drawing up its own school development plan (see **Standards in**

school education and **Education authorities** for further information).

Accessibility strategies may also be timed to coincide with the authority's Children's Services planning cycle. The accessibility strategy is an authority wide document but, in practical terms, individual schools will need to be involved in the preparation and implementation of the strategy.

In preparing an accessibility strategy, the education authority (or independent or grant-aided school) has to have regard to:

- the need to allocate adequate resources for implementing the strategy;
- consultation to be carried out with such children, parents and young people as they think fit;
- Scottish Government guidance.

A copy of an accessibility strategy must be made available to inspect, if requested. The information can be requested in alternative formats.

If a parent or pupil is concerned that the terms of an accessibility strategy are not being complied with, they can make a complaint to the education authority or directly to the Scottish Ministers (in the case of an education authority) or to the governors of the school (in the case of independent or grant-aided schools). The section on **Complaints** gives further information.

See Also

Additional Support for Learning
Complaints
Disability Discrimination
Equal opportunities and equality duties

Useful organisations

Enquire
Equalities and Human Rights Commission
Independent Special Education Advice (Scotland)

Useful publications

Scottish Executive (2002) *Planning to Improve Access to Education for Pupils with Disabilities: Guidance on Preparing Accessibility Strategies* (available from the Scottish Government)

Scottish Executive (2003) *A Report on the First Round of Accessibility Strategies* (available from the Scottish Government)

Legal References Used in this Section

Education (Disability Strategies and Pupils' Educational Records) (Scotland) Act 2002

Education (Disability Strategies) (Scotland) Regulations 2002, as amended

ADDITIONAL SUPPORT FOR LEARNING

Additional Support Needs

A child or young person has additional support needs if, for whatever reason, they require additional support in order to benefit from school education. This includes, in particular, education which is directed to the development of the child or young person's personality, talents and mental and physical abilities to their fullest potential.

Additional support needs includes, in addition to difficulties which stem from medical or disability related factors, other difficulties such as linguistic barriers, marital breakdown, itinerant lifestyles, and social or emotional difficulties. The term also applies to gifted children who require additional support to reach their potential (see **Special aptitudes and abilities**).

The education authority must have appropriate arrangements in place for establishing whether or not any given child or young person has additional support needs.

The authority must establish whether or not the child or young person has additional support needs if:

• they are requested to do so by the parent or young person and that request is not an unreasonable one; or

• a child or young person comes to their attention as having or appearing to have additional support needs.

In providing school education the education authority must have regard to the additional support needs of all children and young people who have such needs.

The education authority must make appropriate arrangements

for keeping under consideration the needs of such children and young people and the adequacy of support provided for them. The education authority must also make adequate and efficient provision for the additional support required by each child or young person with additional support needs, where the authority are responsible for their school education. However, this last duty does not require the education authority to do anything which they do not otherwise have the power to do, nor anything which would result in the authority incurring unreasonable public expenditure.

Education authorities are not normally responsible for the school education of children under the age of 3. However, a Health Board can refer a disabled child under school age, to an education authority. The authority can, but does not have to, establish whether the child has additional support needs resulting from the child's disability. If this is established, the authority has a duty to provide additional support.

Co-ordinated Support Plans

Some children and young people with additional support needs will have a statutory planning document known as a Co-ordinated Support Plan (or CSP) – though most will not. (see **Co-ordinated Support Plans**)

Most rights and obligations under the Additional Support for Learning legislation apply equally, whether there is a CSP or not.

Assessments and examinations

A parent or young person can request a specific type of assessment or examination in three circumstances:

1. Where an education authority is establishing whether a child had additional support needs;

2. Where an education authority is establishing whether a child needs a co-ordinated support plan; or

3. Where an education authority is reviewing a co-ordinated supported plan.

The assessment or examination requested may include educational, psychological or medical assessment or examination, but may also include other forms of assessment. The Code of Practice says that this might include a range of multi-disciplinary assessments. The education authority must comply with an assessment request unless the request is unreasonable. This is not a right to request an assessment by a specific individual, assessments will be carried out by somebody who the authority consider to be appropriate to do so.

If an assessment request is refused, the parent or young person can ask for dispute resolution (see **Dispute resolution**).

Arrangements for children and young people not educated by the education authority

The Additional Support for Leaning Act (2004) says that an education authority are responsible for a child or young person's school education if:

a) they attend a school managed by that authority; or

b) they receive education by virtue of arrangements made or entered into by the authority.

For example, if a child attends an independent special school, but that place is funded by the education authority, the authority remain responsible for the child's school education. If a child is educated at home by their parents, then the authority will not be responsible for that child's school education. If the child is educated at home, but with some support from the education authority, then it will depend on the amount of input and control the authority has in the educational arrangements for the child.

Where the authority are not responsible for a child or young person's school education the parent or young person can request that the authority establish whether or not the child or young person has additional support needs. The authority may comply with such a request but is not obliged to do so. It must exercise this discretion reasonably.

A child or young person is not eligible for a Co-ordinated Support Plan where the authority are not responsible for their school education

Any of the following may make a request that the education authority establish whether a child or young person would require a CSP (if the authority were responsible for their school education):

• the parent or young person concerned; or

• the managers of a grant-aided or independent school attended by the child or young person in question.

Again, the authority have a power, but not a duty, to comply with such a request. This discretion must be exercised reasonably.

Where someone, other than the young person, parents or school managers, draws to the attention of an education authority that a child or young person may have additional support needs, the authority may take action to establish that. The authority would obviously require the consent of the parent or young person to do so.

If the authority establishes that a child or young person does have additional support needs or would, if they were responsible for that child or young person's school education, have required a Co-ordinated Support Plan, then the education authority must provide appropriate advice and information to the parent or young person (or the managers of the independent or grant-aided school).

Education authorities do not have to make provision for supporting the learning of a child or young person who is not in the public schooling system, but they have powers to do so. These discretionary powers must also be exercised reasonably.

Placing requests

Parents (or young people) can make a placing request for a child or young person, with additional support needs, to attend a particular school. A placing request for a child or young person with additional support needs may be for a pre-school placement, a local authority school, an independent or grant-aided special school in Scotland or a special school in England, Wales or Northern Ireland.

As a result of a recent court decision, a placing request cannot be for a child or young person with additional support needs to attend a local authority school outwith the local authority area the parent or young person lives in. The Scottish Government have announced their intention to reverse this decision by legislation and a Bill is expected very shortly.

The education authority must comply with a placing request unless one or more grounds apply for refusing such a request. This includes grounds applicable for all children (see **Choice of School**) as well as certain additional grounds:

• where the specified school is a special school which is not managed by an education authority in Scotland and the child or young person does not have additional support needs requiring the education or special facilities normally provided at that school;

• where the specified school is a special school which is not managed by an education authority in Scotland and:

– the education authority is able to make provision for the additional support needs of the child or young person in another school and;

– the child or young person has been offered a place there and it is not reasonable, considering the respective costs and suitability to place him or her in the specified school;

• where the specified school is a special school and placing the child or young person would breach the education authority's duty to educate all children of school age in mainstream schools (subject to certain exceptions).

See **Choice of School** for more information on placing children with additional support needs in mainstream schools.

Following a successful placing request, where the specified school is not managed by an education authority in Scotland, the education authority to whose area the child or young person belongs must meet all fees and other necessary costs of attendance at that school (e.g. travel, materials etc.).

Appeals against a refusal of a placing request will be heard by the education appeal committee and further appeals by the sheriff, in the normal way (see **Appeals**). However, where a child or young person also has a Co-ordinated Support Plan, or a decision has been taken that they require one (or where the parent or young person is appealing against a decision that they do not require one) the appeal will be heard by the Additional Support Needs Tribunal (see **Appeals**). The rules about whether a placing request appeal should be heard by an appeal committee or a Tribunal are complicated and are due to change shortly, so do take care to check which is the correct route before making an appeal.

School placements outwith the UK

If a child or young person has additional support needs, the education authority has a discretionary power (which is likely to be used only exceptionally) to enable him or her to attend an educational establishment which caters for his or her needs outwith the United Kingdom (e.g. Boston Higashi School in the USA or the Peto Institute in Budapest). Payment may be made for fees and travelling, maintenance and other expenses, for the child and also the child's parent(s) or other person, if their presence would be to the advantage of the child or young person.

Informing and involving parents, young people and children

The Education (Additional Support for Learning) Act 2004 requires education authorities to seek and take account of the views of:

• young people aged 16 and 17, unless the education authority is satisfied that they lack the capacity to express a view;

• children, unless the education authority is satisfied that the child lacks capacity to express a view;

• parents, in the case of children under 16 and young people who lack capacity to express a view.

Views should be taken into account when the education authority are establishing an individual's additional support needs or when determining the provision of support to be made. It should also be done when the authority are establishing whether a co-ordinated support plan is needed, when the need for continuing such a plan is being reviewed or when a plan is being prepared as well as in planning for a child or young person leaving school.

Education authorities must inform a parent or young person of:

• their intentions to consider whether or not a child or young person may require a co-ordinated support plan, or if the plan needs to be reviewed, before proceeding;

• the decision on whether the child or young person requires a co-ordinated support plan, or whether the plan needs to be reviewed;

• any rights they may have to appeal to an Additional Support Needs Tribunal.

When a plan has been prepared, or amended, the education authority must provide a copy of the plan to the parent or young person.

Education authorities must also publish their policies on Additional Support for Learning, including policies on mediation, and review and revise that information when necessary.

Changes in School Education

The education authority must help to plan services for a child or young person with additional support needs who is leaving school. The requirements on education authorities are not restricted to children or young people with co-ordinated support plans, they apply to all children and young people with additional support needs.

The authority must:

• ask for information and advice from agencies likely to support the young person once they have left school and take account of this information. This must be done at least 12 months before the young person leaves school;

• provide information to the agencies which will be responsible for supporting the young person once they leave school (including continuing, further and higher education institutions). This must be done at least 6 months before the child or young person is expected to leave school, but it could be done earlier;

• information may only be given to other agencies with the consent of the child's parent or the young person. Where information has been passed on, education authorities must then inform such other agencies of the actual date when the young person does leave school.

Similarly, there are duties which apply where a child or young person is starting a school for the first time, moving from nursery to primary, or primary to secondary school; or changing school for another reason (e.g. moving house; an exclusion from school etc.).

12 months (6 months for pre-school children) prior to the change in school education (or as soon as possible after the date is known) the education authority must seek relevant advice and information from relevant agencies and people in order to:

• establish what the child or young person's additional support needs are;

• determine what provision for those additional support needs may be required in the new context; and

• consider the adequacy of the additional support currently provided (if any).

The views of the child and parent or young person will be sought if appropriate.

All of the advice and information thus obtained must be taken into account in making appropriate arrangements prior to the change in school education.

No later than six months (three months in the case of pre-school children) prior to the change in school education, (or as soon as possible after the date is known) the authority must pass on relevant information to the appropriate agencies. This may include:

- the likely date of the change in school education;
- the additional support needs of the child or young person; and
- the additional support provided during the previous six months (three months in the case of pre-school children).

Where information is provided in this way, a copy of that information must be also provided to the parent or young person. Information must not be provided to external agencies without consent of the parent or young person.

Supporters and advocacy

Parents and young people have the right to make use of either a supporter or an advocate, in discussions with the education authority about additional support needs or co-ordinated support plans. A supporter is someone who is present during discussions to support the parent or young person. An advocate is someone who would conduct the discussion or make representations to the authority on behalf of a parent or young person.

The education authority must comply with the wishes of a parent or young person to use a supporter or advocate unless their wishes are "unreasonable". Neither the authority, nor anyone else, has a duty to provide or pay for a supporter or advocate.

Resolving disagreements

The Act provides various mechanisms for resolving disputes which may arise between the authority and parents or young people. These are considered elsewhere in the book (see **Appeals**, **Dispute Resolution** and **Mediation**).

Code of Practice

The Scottish Ministers have published a Code of Practice to provide guidance to education authorities and other appropriate agencies on their functions in relation to additional support needs.

The Code of Practice covers:

- circumstances or factors which may give rise to additional support needs;
- the identification of such factors;
- the nature of additional support which may be required by children or young people with additional support needs;
- the nature of additional support to be provided under a co-ordinated support plan;
- arrangements to be made to establish whether children or young people have additional support needs / require co-ordinated support plans;
- the seeking of information, advice and views in certain specified circumstances;
- the arrangements to be made for provision of mediation services;
- placing requests for children or young people with additional support needs.

Education authorities and appropriate agencies must have regard to the terms of the Code of Practice in exercising their functions in relation to additional support needs.

See also

Appeals
Choice of School
Coordinated Support Plans
Dispute Resolution
Mediation

Useful organisations

Additional Support Needs Tribunals
Enquire
Independent Special Education Advice (Scotland)
Parentzone

Useful publications

Enquire (2006) *The Parents Guide to Additional Support for Learning*

Scottish Consumer Council (2006) *Supporting children and young people's learning: a handbook for parents when their child needs additional support* (available from TSO)

Scottish Government (2007) *Education (Additional Support for Learning) (Scotland) Act 2004: A Guide For Parents/Carers*

Legal References Used in this Section

Education (Additional Support for Learning) (Scotland) Act 2004

ADMISSION TO SCHOOL

Nursery school

There is no legal requirement on parents for children under 5 years old to be educated. However, services for both the care and education of pre-school children are provided by voluntary organisations, local authorities and private nurseries, many of which will take children from as young as 6 weeks old. Local Authorities are now under a duty to provide a part-time pre-school place to all children aged 3 and 4 years old (see **Pre-School Education**).

Primary school

Most children are admitted to primary school aged from approx. 4½ years old and transfer to secondary school after completing primary 7 (approx. age 11). Children who are not 5 by the school commencement date in August can either be treated as if they were 5 and admitted to school in that year, or have their entry deferred to the following August, meaning that the August intake takes children from 4 years 6 months to 5 years 6 months (or even 5 years 11 months in a few cases). The education authority must tell all parents whose children are due to start primary school the following session about their local catchment area school. It must also tell parents about their right to choose a different school (see **School starting age)**.

If there were a good reason why a child should start school earlier than usual, a parents can approach the education authority to request that their child admitted early to a primary school. The education authority may only refuse this request if the education provided at that school is not suitable for the child's aptitude and ability.

Parents are under a duty to provide education for their children. They do not, however, have to place them in a school and may wish to educate their children at home (see **Home education**).

Additional support needs

If a child has additional support needs which have been identified at the pre-school stage, the parent(s) should have been involved in discussions about whether the child's needs would be best met at the local primary, and whether additional support is required for their child. The education authority have a duty to educate children in mainstream schools, except in exceptional circumstances (see **Additional Support for Learning**).

Going from primary to secondary

Where a child is due to transfer from primary to secondary school at the start of the following session, their parent(s) will again be told about the local catchment area secondary school, and the right to request a different school. Increasingly primary and secondary schools are working together to smooth the transition between primary and secondary school and therefore your child may attend secondary for a day or more prior to moving up at the end of primary 7.

If a child has additional support needs, there are additional duties on the education authority to provide transitional support prior to the move to secondary school (see **Additional Support for Learning**).

What if a child is not ready for secondary school?

In some circumstances, parents may wish to defer their child's entry to secondary school for a year to allow the child to repeat primary 7, if they feel that the child is not ready to benefit from secondary education. The education authority may suggest this, or a parent may ask the authority to consider it. This is usually treated as a matter of discretion for the authority, but parents may be able to insist upon a child remaining at a school or make a placing request to secure this. The parents of children with additional support needs may be able to refer this matter to mediation or dispute resolution (see **Mediation** and **Dispute resolution**). Parents should discuss their child's progress with the head teacher in the first instance.

If parent(s) are moving house, their children may need to change school. The education authority for the area moved to will provide information about enrolling children in local schools. Again, if parents would prefer their child to attend a different school, they are entitled to make a placing request for another school.

See also

Additional Support for Learning
Choice of school
Dispute resolution
Home education
Mediation
Pre-school education
School starting age

Useful organisations

Enquire
Independent Special Education Advice (Scotland)
Parentzone

Legal references used in this section

Sections 31, 32; Education (Scotland) Act 1980

Education (School and Placing Information) (Scotland) Regulations 1982

Sections 32-38; Standards in Scotland's Schools etc. Act 2000

Provision of School Education for Children under School Age (Prescribed Children) (Scotland) Order 2002

ADVICE AND ASSISTANCE

There are many places that can provide advice and assistance to parents. This section describes some in detail. Information on specific bodies is available in the **Useful organisations** section at the end of this book.

School staff. A child's class, guidance or head teacher will usually be willing to discuss any concerns parents have about their child's schooling. Parents should always try to discuss concerns about how their children are getting on at school (e.g. their children's educational progress or bullying problems) with school staff before taking the matter any further.

Other parents. Sometimes parents can get the information they need just by speaking informally to other parents whose children attend the school. This can be particularly helpful if considering what school to send children to.

Parent Councils or other parents groups. If there is a Parent-Teacher Association, Parent Association or Parent Council at a school, they may be able to offer advice on how to deal with a specific query, or may be able to take up a general issue with the school on behalf of parents.

Education authority officials. If parents need information about the education authority's policies or procedures, they can get this by contacting the relevant section of the education department. Many functions such as additional support for learning, transport to school, grants, bursaries etc. will be dealt with at this level. If parents are unsure of whom to approach within the education authority, the local council central switchboard should be able to direct them to the appropriate person. Similarly, council websites now often provide direct phone numbers to relevant members of staff. The section on **Education authorities** has further information.

Careers office. The local careers office will be able to provide older children and young people with information about employment, training and further and higher education. See the section on **Careers education** for further information.

Local advice centres. Citizens' Advice Bureaux are staffed by volunteers and paid workers and have access to a range of information materials. They provide a free basic advice service on a whole host of different subjects. They may be able to provide general advice on educational matters. They may be able to write letters on behalf of parents and some may offer an advocacy service at appeal committee hearings. Some areas may have other advice services. If there is a local community council, they will be able provide information on what advice services are available in the local area. There may be a youth information service in the local area, which is likely to have information on schools and education.

Voluntary Organisations. Many voluntary organisations are able to provide advice and support to parents, either in general (for example, Parentline Scotland) or in relation to specific issues (for example, Enquire, the national advice service for additional support needs). Further information on such groups is contained in the Further information on such groups is contained in the **Useful organisations** section of this book.

Solicitors. Solicitors will be able to provide more detailed and expert legal advice and representation if necessary. Not all solicitors will deal with education matters, so parents should ask before making an appointment. The Law Society of Scotland has a list of solicitors who have specialist accreditation in child law. They may be more likely to take your case on. Legal advice is available free of charge, or subject to a small contribution to those on low incomes or on benefits, under the Advice and Assistance (A&A) scheme. Many solicitors offer a free first interview, where they will establish whether someone would be eligible for A&A. Representation at education appeal committee hearings is not covered by the A&A scheme, and so parents may be charged a fee for this. If a case needs to go to court, Legal Aid may be available. In some cases, financial eligibility for Legal Aid may be based on the child's income, rather than the parent's.

Law Centres. Law Centres exist to provide free legal advice and representation in areas of unmet legal need, to people living in their areas. If there is a Law Centre in your area, they may be willing to take on an education case. You should contact the Scottish Association of Law Centres to find out if there is a Law Centre in your area. There are also three Law Centres which may be able to provide specialist advice or representation to parents or children anywhere in Scotland. These are the Education Law Unit (based at Govan Law Centre), and cl@n childlaw and the Scottish Child Law Centre (both based in Edinburgh).

Mediation Services. In some education authority areas, mediation services may be available. Mediation is a form of assisted negotiation in which an independent third party (the mediator) helps those involved to reach a mutually acceptable outcome. Parents should ask the education authority for information on any arrangements which they have for mediation. For disputes in relation to additional support needs, mediation will have to be available (see **Additional Support for Learning**).

Publications and internet materials

There are a wide range of books, periodicals and leaflets on education-related topics. Increasingly, materials are available free of charge on the internet. This is probably the quickest and cheapest way to get up to date information. Most of the organisations above produce leaflets for parents and children. There is also a list of **useful organisations** at the end of this book. Parents can find out what leaflets are available by contacting an organisation directly or by checking the organisation's web site if they have one.

Copies of the Scottish Government circulars, guidance and codes of practice are available by contacting the Scottish Government

Directorate for Schools, or can be found on the Scottish Government's website. Copies of Inspectors' reports are available from HM Inspectorate of Education, and on their website. Copies of laws and regulations are available from the Office of Public Sector Information at www.opsi.gov.uk/legislation/. Details of how to contact these organisations are at the end of the book.

Newspapers such as The Scotsman, The Herald and The Guardian have weekly education pages where current education issues are discussed. These papers will also report on any important developments. The Times Educational Supplement (Scotland) may also be useful.

Libraries and bookshops may also have a section on education, which may have books of interest.

See also

Complaints
Guidance
Information for parents
Legal action
Parental involvement and representation

Useful organisations

Childline
Citizens Advice Scotland
Enquire
Govan Law Centre: Education Law Unit
Independent Special Education Advice (Scotland)
Parentline
Parentzone

APPEALS

Parents have appeal rights in certain areas of education law:

• Additional support needs;
• Placing requests;
• Exclusions; and
• Attendance orders.

Who has the right to make an appeal?

Parents have the right of appeal in all cases where their child is still under school leaving age (16 years old). They may also have the right of appeal in cases where their child is over that age (i.e. is a young person), but the young person does not have the necessary understanding to appeal on their own.

However, generally once pupils are over school leaving age, they will have the right of appeal and their parent(s) will not.

In exclusion appeals, if a child is of sufficient maturity and understanding but under school leaving age, both parent and child have the right to appeal. It is presumed that a child aged 12 or over has such maturity and understanding.

What decisions can be appealed?

There are only certain decisions which can be appealed:

• exclusion from school;
• the making or amendment of an attendance order;
• refusal of a placing request;
• opening a Co-ordinated Support Plan or continuing a CSP on review;

- refusing to open a CSP or discontinuing it on review;
- failure to comply with certain time limits connected with a CSP;
- certain information contained within a CSP.

Exclusion appeals and most appeals against placing request refusals are heard by the education appeal committee, with a further right of appeal to the Sheriff. Appeals against an attendance order are heard by the Sheriff. Appeals in relation to Co-ordinated Support Plans (including some placing request appeals) are heard by the Additional Support Needs Tribunal.

The education appeal committee

Appeals about most placing requests and all exclusions are heard by an education appeal committee, set up and maintained by the education authority. Education appeal committees are supervised by the Administrative Justice & Tribunals Council (Scottish Committee).

An appeal committee can have three, five or seven members. These will be councillors from the local authority, parents (taken from Parent Councils, attendance councils etc.), and others with a knowledge of local educational matters. The councillors must not outnumber the other members by more than one. The chair must not be a councillor from the Council's education committee. None of the members should be involved in the school which the child attends (or has made a placing request to).

The appeal committee must tell the appellant (the person who is appealing) when the date for the hearing will be within 14 days of receiving the appeal, and must give at least 14 days warning of the hearing. The hearing must usually be within 28 days of receiving an appeal letter.

The appellant has the following rights at an appeal:

- the right to appear and be represented;
- the right to be accompanied by up to three people (including a representative or advocate, if any); and

- the right to submit a written case, as well as, or instead of, speaking to the committee.

The appeal hearing will usually go in this order:

- the education authority will present its arguments;
- the appellant can question any of the authority's witnesses;
- the appellant will present his or her arguments;
- the appellant and/or his or her witnesses can be questioned;
- the education authority will sum up; and finally
- the appellant have a chance to sum up.

However, the chair of the committee has ultimate control over the procedure followed. The committee members are also allowed to put questions to anyone giving evidence at the hearing.

The appeal committee must take into account all relevant matters in making its decision. These should include those set out in their Code of Practice.

The appeal committee must give its decision in writing within 14 days, together with the reasons for their decision. The decision should be detailed enough so that the appellant is able to understand why the decision was taken. If unsuccessful, appellants must be told about their rights of further appeal to the Sheriff court.

"Adequate" reasons should be given, although a lack of reasons does not affect the validity of a decision under appeal.

The education authority has no right of further appeal from the education appeal committee, but a legal challenge may lie by way of judicial review in certain circumstances.

"Deemed decisions"

If an appeal committee has:

- not heard an appeal within one month (for exclusions) or two months (for placing requests); or
- fails to give a written decision within fourteen days of the hearing

then it is *deemed* in law to have decided the case against the appellant (i.e. in favour of the education authority). This allows the appellant to take advantage of his or her further right of appeal to the Sheriff.

Appeals to the sheriff court

For any appeal heard by the education appeal committee, the appellant has a right of further appeal to the Sheriff court. The appeal must be made within 28 days (or later if there is a good reason for the delay) by way of "summary application". Appeals against an attendance order go directly to the Sheriff court.

For placing requests, the appeal is a complete rehearing of the case. For exclusion cases, the court will hear evidence on whether or not the decision to exclude was justified. For attendance order appeals, the court will decide whether the education authority exercised its discretion properly or not.

An appeal to the Sheriff court, while kept as informal as possible, is a complex legal procedure. Parents, children or young people should seek legal advice and representation, from a solicitor familiar with education law. The appellant may be entitled to Legal Aid, but this will be assessed on the parent's income and capital (unless the child or young person is bringing the court action on their own – e.g. a child over 12 appealing against their own exclusion, or a young person appealing against a refusal of a placing request they made).

The decision of the Sheriff in each case is final, and there is no right of appeal. However, in some limited circumstances, the Sheriff's decision can be challenged by way of judicial review in the Court of Session.

Additional Support Needs Tribunals for Scotland

Each Additional Support Needs Tribunal comprises of 1 legally qualified convener sitting together with 2 wing members with professional experience of additional support needs.

The Tribunal is subject to an "overriding objective", which is to deal with references fairly and justly. That includes:

- dealing with appeals in a way which is proportionate to the complexity of the case;
- seeking informality and flexibility in the proceedings;
- trying to make sure that the parties are on an equal footing (this may include assisting a parent or young person to present their case);
- using their special expertise effectively; and
- avoiding delay, where possible.

Parents and young people can refer certain matters relating to co-ordinated support plans to an Additional Support Needs Tribunal. The matters that may be referred to the Tribunal are:

- a decision of the education authority that a child or young person requires (or, on review, still requires) a Co-ordinated Support Plan;
- a decision of the education authority that a child or young person does not require (or, on review, no longer requires) a Co-ordinated Support Plan;
- a failure of the education authority to prepare a plan in the specified time limit;
- any of the education authority's conclusions contained in the plan as to:
  - the factors giving rise to the additional support needs;
  - the educational objectives for the child or young person;
  - the additional support required to achieve those objectives; and/or
  - the people or agencies who will provide the additional support.
- a failure by the education authority to commence a review of a plan;
- a failure to complete the review process within the specified time limit; and
- a refusal to review a plan on request from the parent or young person.

Placing requests appeals will be heard by a Tribunal only where, at the time of the refusal of the placing request:

- the child or young person has a co-ordinated support plan; or
- it has been established that the child or young person requires a plan but the plan has not yet been prepared; or
- it has been established that the child or young person does not require a plan and that decision is also being appealed to an ASN Tribunal.

If a placing request appeal is being dealt with by the education appeal committee or Sheriff, and a reference is lodged with the Tribunal appealing against a decision of the education authority that a child or young person does not require a CSP, then this has the effect of transferring the placing request appeal to the Tribunal as well.

If the Tribunal confirms on appeal that a child or young person does not require a CSP, any placing request appeal also with the Tribunal is referred to the education appeal committee for determination.

The rules about which the type of appeals can be heard by Tribunal (including possible new rights of appeal) and under what circumstances an appeal might transfer from an appeal committee or Sheriff to the Tribunal are due to change shortly. You should therefore be careful to check whether you have a right of appeal and, if so, to which body that appeal should be made.

The Tribunal has considerable powers to confirm or overturn decisions made by the education authority. The Tribunal may also require the education authority to take appropriate actions with set time limits, in order to rectify failures on the part of the authority. In relation to information contained in a co-ordinated support plan, the Tribunal may confirm the information or require the authority to amend the information within a set time limit. Placing request appeals are determined by the Tribunal on the same basis as before the education appeal committee or Sheriff court (see above and the section on Choice of School).

The Tribunal has powers to compel the recovery of documents and the attendance of relevant witnesses. It is a criminal offence to fail, without reasonable excuse, to produce the documents requested or attend as a witness once cited. The Tribunal has powers to allow evidence to be heard by telephone, video link or other means, if necessary. The Tribunal may also appoint an expert witness to give evidence or prepare a report.

No Legal Aid is available for proceedings before the Tribunal. However, both parents (or young persons) and education authorities are entitled to be represented.

See also

Additional Support for Learning
Attendance and absence
Choice of school
Complaints
Exclusion from school
Legal action
Scottish Parliament and the Scottish Government

Useful organisations

Additional Support Needs Tribunals
Enquire
Independent Special Education Advice (Scotland)
Parentzone

Useful publications

CoSLA (1988) *Code of Practice for Constitution and Procedures of Education Appeal Committees in Scotland* (1988)

Scottish Committee of the Council on Tribunals (2000) *Special Report on Education Appeal Committee* (available from the Administrative Justice and Tribunals Committee at www.ajtc.gov.uk)

Scottish Consumer Councils (2006) *Complaints in Education* (available from Consumer Focus Scotland)

Scottish Executive (2007) *Education Appeal Committees Proposals for Reform* (available from the Scottish Government)

Legal references used in this section

Section 41 of the Standards in Scotland's Schools etc. (Scotland) Act 2000

Sections 28D, 28E, 28F, 28H Schedule A1; Education (Scotland) Act 1980

Sections 4, 10, Schedule 1, Part II, para 50(b) of the Tribunals and Inquiries Act 1992

Education (Appeal Committee Procedures) (Scotland) Regulations 1982

Reg. 5; Education (Placing in Schools) (Scotland) Regulations 1982

Sections 1, 3, 6; Human Rights Act 1998

Campbell and Cosans v. United Kingdom (1982) 4 EHRR 293

Wallace v. Dundee City Council 2000 SLT (Sh Ct) 60

Glasgow City Council v. Fox-Flynn 4 Jan 2004, Court of Session (Outer House)

ATTENDANCE AND ABSENCE

Attendance at school

There is no *duty* on children to attend school or on their parents to send them to school. What the law requires is that parents provide their school-aged children (roughly age 5-16 but see section on **Admission to school** and **School starting ag**e with efficient education suitable to his or her age, ability and aptitude. This can be provided by sending their children to a local authority school or by some other means. "Other means" includes educating children at home or sending them to an independent school (see **Home Education** and **Independent Schools**).

Parents have a legal obligation to seek their child's views when making important decisions such as choosing a particular type of education.

Once a child is registered and attends a local authority school, parents must ensure that he or she attends regularly. If a parent wants to withdraw their child from school, then they must ask for the education authority's consent. The education authority must not unreasonably withhold that consent.

Exemptions from school attendance

In exceptional circumstances, the parents of children over 14 may ask the education authority to exempt their child from attending school for the rest of that school session, in order for the child to help out at home. This would only be granted if the child's home circumstances meant that it would cause "exceptional hardship" if the child had to attend school. If the exemption is granted because of the illness or infirmity of a member of the child's family, then, as far as practicable and without undue delay, the education authority must make special arrangements for the child to receive education out of school.

Absence from school

Once children are registered at and attend a local authority school, they must attend regularly, unless there is a *reasonable excuse* for absence. There is a reasonable excuse if:

- a child cannot attend school or receive education because of illness (the education authority may arrange for a child to be medically examined in this situation, and parents may, in theory, be prosecuted if they do not allow such an examination to take place);
- a child lives further than the statutory walking distance from school (see **Transport**); or
- there are other circumstances which would count as a reasonable excuse.

Scottish Goverment guidance on attendance and absence suggests that the following circumstances may constitute a reasonable excuse:

- medical or dental appointments;
- family bereavement;
- short-term exceptional circumstances at home;
- special religious holidays;
- meetings prior to and in court;
- attendance at or in connection with a Children's Hearing (see **Children's hearings**) or Care Review;
- family weddings; and
- sanctioned extended absence for children of travelling families (see **Travellers inc. Gypsy/Travellers**).

This is not an exhaustive list.

If a pupil is absent from school due to ill health, the education authority must make special arrangements for the pupil to receive education elsewhere (e.g. at home or in hospital). Scottish Government guidance suggests that there should be an automatic referral by schools for education outwith school after 15 working days of continuous absence or 20 working days of intermittent absence, for verifiable medical reasons.

Absence without reasonable excuse

If the education authority suspect that parents have failed to make sure their child attends school regularly, without reasonable excuse, it can call the parents to a meeting to discuss the reasons for the child's non-attendance (this is usually called an attendance council). The attendance council has the power to:

- refer the child to the to the children's panel (see **Children's hearings**);
- make an "attendance order" requiring the child to attend his or her local school and/or;
- decide that a parent should be prosecuted.

Prosecution for failing to ensure a child attends school is, in practice, unusual, and is generally only used in cases where other measures have been tried first.

If a parent does not agree with an attendance order, they can appeal against it to the Sheriff Court within 14 days of the date the order was served. Parents appealing against an attendance order should seek legal advice from a solicitor experienced in education law matters. Legal Aid may be available.

See also

Appeals
Children's hearings
Health
Home education
Independent schools
Transport
Travellers inc. Gypsy/Travellers

Useful organisations

Childline
Parentline

Parentzone

Schoolhouse Home Education Association

Useful publications

Scottish Government (2007) *Included, Engaged and Involved Part 1: Guidance on the management of attendance and absence in Scottish Schools* (available from the Scottish Government)

Legal references used in this section

Sections 14, 30, 34, 35, 36, 42; Education (Scotland) Act 1980 (as amended)

Section 6; Children (Scotland) Act 1995

BOARDING ACCOMMODATION

The education authority must provide boarding accommodation if:

- the nearest suitable school is too far for a child to travel to on a daily basis;
- the child's home is very remote; or
- there are other exceptional circumstances which mean a child would be unable to receive the full benefit of school education unless boarding accommodation was provided.

A child may attend a particular school outwith their local catchment area, because of a parental placing request. If so, the education authority *may* provide boarding accommodation but it is not under any obligation to do so.

However, a child with additional support needs may be placed in an independent or grant-aided special school in Scotland or a special school in England, Wales or Northern Ireland as a result of a parental placing request. Where this happens, the education authority would need to meet the fees and other necessary costs of attendance. If the school is a residential school, then this may include boarding costs. Education authorities have the power to arrange for children to be educated outwith the UK, though this is exceptional. See **Additional Support for Learning** for further information.

Accommodation may be provided in a boarding school, hostel, children's home or other institution, or with a family or individual. If the accommodation is with a family or individual, parents have the right to request that the "host family" are of a particular religious denomination. The education authority must meet that request, as far as is reasonably practicable.

When the education authority is making arrangements for a child to receive boarding accommodation, it must consult the child's parent(s). There is also an obligation on the parent to take account of the child's views on the matter.

While a child is being accommodated under these provisions, the education authority has a duty to safeguard and promote the child's welfare, and has the right to carry out inspections to ensure that the child's welfare is adequately safeguarded and promoted. Inspections are also carried out by HM Inspectorate of Education and the Care Commission.

Who pays?

Where accommodation must be provided by the education authority for the purpose of school education (as above), the authority cannot charge for the cost of board and lodging and must also provide for any necessary travel or reimburse the cost of the child's travel to and from the accommodation. In other circumstances, the authority may recover all or part of the costs from the parent or young person, provided that they are able to pay those costs without financial hardship.

Religious observance in boarding accommodation

If parents wish their child to attend religious worship or receive religious instruction outwith school hours, the education authority must make reasonable arrangements for this, provided it incurs no additional expenditure as a result.

See also

Additional Support for Learning
Choice of school
Inspections and inspector's reports
Religious education and observance

Useful organisations

Care Commission

Childline (which has a dedicated helpline for children and young people living away from home)

HM Inspectorate of Education

Useful publications

Scottish Executive (2005) *National Care Standards: School Care Accommodation Services* (available from the Scottish Government)

Legal references used in this section

Sections 10, 50, 52; Education (Scotland) Act 1980

Schedule 2; Education (Additional Support for Learning) (Scotland) Act 2004

BOOKS, EQUIPMENT AND MATERIALS

School books and materials

Pupils in education authority schools must be provided, free of charge, with any books, writing materials, stationery, mathematical instruments, practice material and other items which are necessary for the course of study being followed.

Schools are allocated a budget for materials and have a certain amount of discretion in what is provided, within education authority guidelines. Schools sometimes fundraise or ask for donations to cover the costs of books and other materials, often through Parent-Teacher Associations, Parents' Associations or Parent Councils, but it is unlawful to require payment from either parent or child for essential articles.

Sponsorship

Increasingly, schools are raising funds for school books and sports equipment through sponsorship arrangements with private companies. There is no legislation covering what can and cannot be sponsored. However, the Scottish Consumer Council (now Consumer Focus Scotland) produced guidelines on sponsorship in schools covering the principles of best practice.

Damage to books, equipment and materials

Necessary articles provided by the school free of charge will remain the property of the education authority and may have to remain within the school buildings. If a child is allowed to take school books or other items home, then he or she is responsible for taking care of them and may have to pay if they are damaged (beyond reasonable wear and tear).

Resources for additional support needs

Pupils with additional support needs may need particular books, resources or equipment which are not ordinarily required by pupils. This could include large print or audio versions of textbooks, specialist computer software, visual aids and symbols etc. The education authority have a duty to provide such resources in order to meet a pupil's additional support needs, unless it would involve unreasonable levels of public expenditure.

Independent schools

If a child attends an independent or fee-paying school, the parent will have to pay for books and materials, either as part of the fees or separately, unless the school fees are met by the education authority.

See also

Additional Support for Learning
Property loss and damage

Useful organisations

Learning and Teaching Scotland
Scottish Parent Teacher Council

Useful publications

Consumer Focus Scotland (2008) *Guidelines on Commercial Sponsorship in the Public Sector*

Scottish Consumer Council (2004) *Guidelines on Commercial Activities in Schools* (available through Consumer Focus Scotland)

Legal references used in this section

Sections 11, 12; Education (Scotland) Act 1980

Section 4; Education (Additional Support for Learning) (Scotland) Act 2004

BULLYING

What is bullying?

There is no legal definition of bullying, but it is generally agreed that it can include: physical violence; threats and intimidation; verbal abuse, insults and teasing; spreading rumours or gossiping; ignoring people or leaving them out; as well as stealing. Some schools would also say that bullying involves repeated incidents against the same victim and is one-sided. Children can be seriously affected by bullying. It can lead to anxiety, distress, illness, absenteeism and difficulties with school work.

Bullying can happen in any school. It is estimated that around 50% of pupils will be victims of bullying at some stage in their schooling. Children can be seriously affected by bullying. It can lead to anxiety, distress, illness, absenteeism and affect educational development. Bullying has many guises but verbal and psychological bullying can be every bit as damaging as cuts and bruises.

What is the school's responsibility?

The education authority must provide an "adequate and efficient" education for children in its area. Where education is provided by the authority, it has a duty to make sure that the education is "directed to the development of the personality, talents and mental and physical abilities" of each child or young person to his or her fullest potential.

If a child is suffering academically as a result of bullying, then the education authority may require to take action in order to fulfil these duties. The most effective way of doing this would most often be to try and resolve the bullying problem, although other measures of support may also be needed. A child may have additional support needs as a result of being bullied, and require additional support in order to benefit from school education (see **Additional Support for Learning**).

The education authority must also take reasonable care for the safety of pupils under its charge.

What about independent schools?

All schools, including independent schools, have to take reasonable care for the safety and health of children in their charge and to exercise care and forethought, and not to subject them to harm.

Independent schools are not, however, bound by the same statutory duties as education authorities (as detailed above). Parents are in a contractual relationship with the school. There may or may not be an express condition that the school will take steps to protect their pupils from bullying. However there may be a term, implied by law, that the school will take reasonable steps to ensure a safe environment in which to learn. This is especially so where the school has adopted a written anti-bullying strategy, as is recommended by the Scottish Council of Independent Schools. A failure to follow that strategy might amount to a breach of contract.

What does the school have to do?

In responding to bullying, schools must act reasonably to try and protect children. What is reasonable is judged by reference to normal practice among schools in anti-bullying. There are Scottish Government guidelines which indicate what this normal practice is (or should be).

The Scottish Executive provided all Scottish schools with two anti-bullying packs (produced in the early 1990s, details in the further reading section). These anti-bullying packs are still the principal guides for schools in this field. Both strongly recommend that each school has an individual, specific anti-bullying policy. HM Inspectorate of Education also now expects schools to have such a policy statement.

Many local authorities have also produced their own materials and/or employed key staff to assist schools with bullying problems.

An anti-bullying policy should outline how the issue will be raised within the school's curriculum, and how incidents will be dealt with after they happen. To be effective, it should involve pupils, parents, teachers and other staff.

Bullying of all kinds should be opposed in schools. There should be a clear message (both in the words of the policy, in its implementation and in the ethos of the school) that bullying is wrong, and will not be tolerated. In some examples, a punitive approach is rejected as ineffective or inappropriate. Children who bully others may need as much help as their victims. Schools are increasingly adopting no-blame and peer-mediation strategies for resolving problems. The aim is to reduce the level of bullying and improve the learning environment for all pupils.

A failure to follow the guidelines on anti-bullying policies, or failure to follow a policy which has been drawn up may amount to a breach of a duty owed by the school to its pupils.

What can parents do?

If a parent becomes aware that their child is being bullied, it is essential to encourage the child to tell the teacher, and for the parent to tell the teacher. If the response is unsatisfactory, then the headteacher should be informed, and if there is still a problem then the education authority should be contacted. However, it may take some time to investigate and resolve bullying properly. Parents who become aware of bullying of others' children, should also inform the school.

When a child has been bullied, the parent's main interest is generally to enable the child to deal with the situation confidently and to recover their self-esteem. If the child needs help to do this, they may have additional support needs. If so, the school should plan to support the child and communicate progress with the parent.

Parents should also be aware when their own child may be bullying others. Bullying behaviour may be an expression of a range of other difficulties or feelings their child is finding hard to handle. Parents can also legitimately seek help from the school to support the child to manage their behaviour and resolve and underlying difficulties.

Can parents keep their children off school?

When a child is being seriously bullied, parents weigh up their obligation to protect their children with their duty to ensure their child attends school and in very extreme circumstances parents may be justified in keeping the child off school. Absence from school cannot be justified in this way if the school has not been told of the bullying or those responsible for the bullying have not been identified. Bullying would only be regarded as a reasonable excuse for non–attendance at school where there was a serious and immediate risk of harm to the child and the school were unwilling or unable to protect the child.

In withdrawing a child from school under these circumstances, there is a likelihood that the education authority would seek to refer the matter to the children's reporter or the attendance council (see **Attendance and absence**).

The case law involving bullying in schools has stressed that full co-operation with the school by both child and parent(s) is essential. In particular, the courts have taken the view that the child must tell the school about the bullying, and continue to tell until the bullying stops. This is often extremely difficult for children. However, if neither parent nor child tells, then the school or education authority may be unable to stop the bullying.

Should the police be involved?

Bullying can involve things such as assault, harassment, intimidation, extortion and theft. These are offences, for all children over the age of criminal responsibility (which is 8 years old in Scotland). All such incidences should be reported to the police. In some areas, schools and the police are now working together to combat and prevent bullying. If the school has not reported the matter, then the child's parent may do so. If a child has been injured, he or she should be taken to see a medical practitioner so that the injuries can be recorded. If there are witnesses to the incident, the police should be asked to note their statements. As with all bullying, the school should also have kept an independent record of the incident.

Legal action

If a child is the victim of verbal or physical abuse at school, then they may be able to bring court action directly against the person(s) responsible for the bullying. The court may grant an interdict and, if it is necessary to protect the child from the risk of further abuse, also attach a power of arrest. This means that the police can arrest the person without warrant where they are suspected to be breaking (or about to break) the terms of the interdict (e.g. by threatening or attacking the child).

Where the school or education authority is negligent in its attempts to protect a child from bullying, it may be legally responsible for any reasonably foreseeable consequences. This means that the child could take legal action seeking compensation for any injuries (including psychological, emotional or financial injury) sustained as a result of the negligence. However, it is very difficult to demonstrate negligence and there has never been a successful case of this sort in the Scottish courts. Legal advice should be sought as soon as possible. Legal Aid may be available.

Advice and Support

There are a number of agencies who specialise in providing advice and support to children and their families when faced with bullying. The Anti-Bullying Network has been set up by the Scottish Executive at the University of Edinburgh, so that teachers, parents and young people can share ideas about how bullying should be tackled. They have a helpline which offers:

- information on how to tackle bullying;
- information on where to go for advice – the Infoline is not itself a counselling or mediation service.

For children and young people, the ChildLine Scotland Bullying helpline may be helpful, there are also some resources on the web.

See **Useful addresses and contacts** for further information on both the Anti-Bullying Network and Childline.

See also

Additional Support for Learning
Attendance and absence
Complaints
Independent schools
Legal action
Safety and supervision

Useful organisations

Antibullying Network
Childline (which has a dedicated freephone bullying helpline for children and young people who are experiencing bullying)
Parentline
Parentzone
respectme

Useful publications

Munn, P. (ed) (1999) *Promoting Positive Behaviour* (available from the Antibullying Network)

Respectme (undated) *Cyberbullying: Are you switched on?*

Respectme (undated) *Pointers for Parents*

Scottish Executive (2005) *Confident Happy Children: Advice for Parents and Carers of Primary School Children on Bullying* (available from the Scottish Government)

Scottish Executive (2005) *Good to Know: Advice for Parents and Carers of Teenagers on Bullying* (available from the Scottish Government)

Legal references used in this section

Section 1; Education (Scotland) Act 1980

Section 2; Standards in Scotland's Schools etc. (Scotland) Act 2000

Schools (Safety and Supervision of Pupils) (Scotland) Regulations 1990

Sections 1, 4; Education (Additional Support for Learning) (Scotland) Act 2004

Skeen v. Tunnah 1970 SLT (Sh. Ct.) 66

Montgomery v. Cumming; (unreported, 17 December 1998, High Court of Justiciary)

Scott v. Lothian Regional Council 1999 RepLR 15

Protection from Abuse (Scotland) Act 2001

CAREERS EDUCATION

The purpose of careers education is to provide those leaving education with information about:

- what jobs or further training may be available to them;
- what further training or education is needed for certain jobs; and
- making applications for work, education and training.

There is a requirement to make the careers service available to those in "relevant education" although it may be made available to those in other types of education, who are unemployed or who are already in work. *Relevant* education includes school education and some college courses (whether part or full time) but does not include higher education. Most higher education institutions will have their own careers service.

Transition from school

For children and young people with additional support needs, Careers Scotland may be one of the appropriate agencies consulted as part of a pupil's transition planning prior to leaving school (see **Additional Support for Learning**).

See also

Additional Support for Learning
Guidance / pastoral care

Useful organisations

Careers Scotland
Learn Direct Scotland
Learning and Teaching Scotland

Parentzone

Skill Scotland

Universities and Colleges Admission Services (UCAS)

Where to find out more

Careers Scotland www.careers-scotland.org.uk

Legal references used in this section

Sections 8-10A; Employment and Training Act 1973 (as amended)

CHILDREN'S HEARINGS

Children's Hearings decide whether the children referred to them need any compulsory measures of supervision from the local authority. The hearing is made up of three volunteers – "panel members" – who receive specialist training before their appointment and throughout their service.

Scotland's Children's Hearings System was set up in the 1970s and in 2004 the (then) Scottish Executive announced a review of the system. The Scottish Government have announced their intention to introduce a Children's Hearings Bill to the Scottish Parliament, which will significantly alter the position described below. You can check www.childrens-hearings.co.uk for the up-to-date position.

Grounds for referral to a children's hearing

Children can be referred to a children's hearing for one or more of the following reasons (or "grounds for referral"):

- they are beyond parental control;
- they are falling into bad associations or are exposed to moral danger;
- their parents are unable to offer them an appropriate level of care (it is worth noting that in the case of young children whose parents are failing to ensure they are attending school regularly without reasonable excuse, this may be also be viewed as a lack of parental care);
- they have been the victim of a "Schedule 1 offence" (e.g. physical or sexual abuse or assault; neglect), or are living as part of the same household as another child who has been

the victim of such an offence or as someone who has committed such an offence;

- they have failed to attend school regularly without reasonable excuse;
- they have committed an offence;
- they have misused solvents, alcohol or drugs.

The Reporter to the Children's Panel

The Reporter to the Children's Panel is the person who decides whether a child should be referred to a children's hearing or not. Anyone who suspects that a child falls into one of the above categories can refer them to the Reporter. When the Reporter receives a referral on a child, the Reporter will begin an investigation into the child's circumstances, in order to establish:

- whether one or more of the grounds for referral exists;
- whether there is a need for support from the local authority in dealing with any difficulties which may be affecting the child; and
- whether this support is required on a compulsory (as opposed to voluntary) basis.

It is only if the answer to all three of these questions is 'yes' that the Reporter will refer a child to a Children's Hearing.

Social background reports

In order to arrive at his or her decision, the Reporter may request a variety of reports. In a large number of cases, the Reporter will request a report from the child's school initially, and may also ask a social worker to visit to provide a report on the child's home circumstances. This "social background report" will outline what local authority support a child and family may benefit from, and will provide an assessment of whether they are willing and able to accept these on a voluntary basis. The Reporter will usually advise a child's parent(s) that the Reporter are investigating a child's case. Both parent and child may give the Reporter their views about what should happen, to help the Reporter make the best decision for the child.

What information does the Children's Hearing receive?

The children's hearing will receive a copy of the grounds for referral, the school report, the social background report and any other reports which may be relevant to the child's case. If the parent and/or child have given the Reporter their views, then the panel members will also receive copies of those views.

The child's parents and main carers will receive a copy of all the papers which the panel members receive. Children, however, currently have no legal right to see the papers, although in practice, many social workers will go through the social background report with the child prior to the hearing.

Initial referral to the Children's Hearing

Both parent and child (if he or she is not presently subject to a supervision requirement) will be sent a copy of the grounds for referral. These set out the legal basis for the child's referral to the hearing, and will include a statement of the facts the Reporter believes back up this legal basis.

At the beginning of the hearing, the chairperson will read out the grounds for referral, with the statement of facts, and will ask if the parent(s) and child understand and accept them.

The hearing cannot proceed to a full discussion about the case until both parent(s) and child accept the grounds for referral. If either parent(s) or child do not accept them, or if the child is too young to understand them, then the hearing must make a decision either to:

• refer the case to the sheriff court for proof; or
• take no further action and dismiss the case on these grounds for referral.

Referral to the Sheriff court for proof

If the hearing decides to refer the case to the Sheriff court for proof, the Reporter will lead evidence from witnesses whom (s)he believes will support the grounds for referral. The parent(s) and/or the child can also call witnesses and lead evidence to show whether the grounds for referral should or should not be established by the Sheriff.

At the end of the court case, the Sheriff will decide whether the grounds for referral are established, based on the evidence and legal arguments he or she has heard. If the Sheriff finds that the grounds have been established, he or she will refer the case back to another children's hearing. If the Sheriff finds that the grounds for referral have not been established, he or she will take no further action and will dismiss the case on those grounds for referral.

Legal Aid is available for this part of the proceedings, and legal advice should be sought if the parent or child is uncertain about the implications of the grounds for referral.

What happens at the Children's Hearing?

If the grounds for referral have been accepted or established, the Children's Hearing will go on to discuss the case in detail, with a view to deciding whether the child needs compulsory measures of supervision.

Usually, the social worker who compiled the social background report will be present. The child's head teacher or guidance teacher may also be present. The hearing will discuss all of the issues fully with everyone who is present. They will ask the parent(s) and child for their views, and must take these into account before making their decision.

It can be worthwhile for both parent and child to spend some time before the hearing thinking about and writing down what they would like to happen and why. This can be passed to the panel members before the hearing and can help make sure that nothing is missed out at the hearing. If the parent does this, then as well as being given to the panel members these written views will also be passed to certain other people attending the hearing, although not to the child.

At the end of the discussion, the hearing has to make a decision about whether the child needs compulsory measures of supervision. Occasionally, they may feel they do not have enough information at that time to make a proper decision, and they will continue the case to another day for further information. The Children's Hearing can make one of the following decisions:

- dismiss the case completely. They will do this if they feel that the child and family do not need any assistance from the local authority, or that if they do, it can be arranged voluntarily, and that no compulsion is necessary; or
- make the child subject to a supervision requirement. This would only be in cases where local authority assistance is required, and the hearing feels that this would not be effective unless it was made compulsory.

Each panel member must give their decision and the reasons for their decision in turn. The decision is reached by majority vote. After the hearing, the parent will be sent out the reasons in writing.

Safeguarders

In some cases the hearing may wish to appoint a safeguarder. Safeguarders are people who are appointed to safeguard the interests of the child in the hearing. This only happens when the hearing feels that they require a report from an independent source as to what is in the child's best interests. The safeguarder will speak with the child and their parents and with the professionals who are submitting reports to the hearing before submitting their recommendations, they will normally attend the hearing.

All 32 local authorities in Scotland have a duty to recruit and maintain a panel of safeguarders, so that a sufficient number is available to meet the need in their area.

What is a supervision requirement?

A supervision requirement is the legal document which says that the child is entitled and obliged to receive assistance from the local authority. It may have conditions attached which require the child to stay away from home (e.g. with relatives, in foster care, a children's home or residential school).

Legal Aid is not generally available for children's hearings, but if the child's liberty is at risk (i.e. the children's hearing may impose a residential supervision order) or it is required to allow the child to effectively participate in the hearing, then a lawyer may be appointed to represent the child.

The vast majority of children who are subject to a supervision requirement remain at home, and it is only as a last resort that children will be removed from home. There may also be conditions attached relating to the child's regular attendance at school or nursery, or about who he or she can have contact with.

A supervision requirement cannot last for more than 12 months without being reviewed by a children's hearing. If either parent or child would like a hearing to review a case earlier than this, they can ask the reporter to arrange a review hearing anytime after 3 months since the last hearing. The local authority can also ask for a review hearing at any time if they feel the child's case should be looked at again. In some cases the panel members may ask that a particular case is brought back to a hearing within the 12 months. They will say this when they are giving their decision and will specify when the hearing should take place.

Appeal

If either parent or child do not agree with the hearing's decision, they can appeal against it to the Sherrif court. An appeal must be lodged in court within 21 days of the hearing's decision. Legal advice should be sought as soon as possible. Legal Aid is available for appeals to the Sherrif court.

See also

Looked after children
Secure residential schools

Useful organisations

Parentline
Parentzone
Scottish Government
(http://www.childrens-hearings.co.uk/infofamilies.asp)

Useful publications

Asquith, Stewart (Ed) (1995) *The Kilbrandon Report: Children and Young Persons Scotland* (available on the Children's Hearings website www.childrens-hearings.co.uk)

Scottish Committee of the Council on Tribunals (2002) *Special Report on the Children's Hearings System* (available from the Administrative Justice and Tribunals Council at www.ajtc.gov.uk)

Scottish Executive (2005) *Being a Witness a Booklet for Children in Childrens Hearing Court Proceedings* (available from the Scottish Government)

Legal references used in this section

Sections 39 to 75; Children (Scotland) Act 1995

Children's Hearings (Legal Representation) (Scotland) Rules 2001 (SSI 2001/ No. 478), as amended by the Children's Hearings (Legal Representation) (Scotland) Amendment Rules 2002 (SSI 2002/ No. 30)

CHOICE OF SCHOOL (including placing requests)

In principle, children should be educated in accordance with their parents wishes. This means that parents may choose to educate their children at home, or to send them to an independent school, for example. If a parent chooses to send their children to a local authority school, then they have the right to choose which one to send their children to. A young person who has the necessary capacity and understanding can make a placing request for him or herself. However, the right to make a placing request is subject to a number of important restrictions.

Choosing an education authority school

The education authority decides on the "catchment areas" for each of its primary and secondary schools. These are largely based on the geographical area where parents live, and in the case of secondary schools, certain primary schools may be "feeder" schools for particular secondaries. During the year before a child is due to start primary school or transfer to secondary school, the education authority will contact their parent(s) telling them about the local school. It will also tell them about their right to make a "placing request" for their child to go to a different school instead, and will give a date by which any placing request must be made. The education authority must also place newspaper adverts telling parents about their right to make a placing request.

Education authorities must publish (or otherwise make available) information about their arrangements for placing children in their schools

Parents have the right to request information on particular schools from the education authority. They can ask for this information from their own education authority, and also from other authorities whose schools they may be interested in. When making a major decision affecting their children, parents are obliged to consult their children, so available options should be discussed with the child.

(NB: where appropriate, this section should be read in conjunction with the **Additional Support for Learning** section as there are special rules for children with additional support needs.)

Presumption of "Mainstreaming"

The education authority have a duty to educate children of school age (and pre-school age) in mainstream schools, rather than special schools. This duty does not apply to children who receive education somewhere other than at a school (e.g. supported home tuition, social work educational provision etc.). Nor does the duty apply where one of the following three exceptions occur:

- the education provided in a mainstream school would not be suitable for the aptitude and abilities of the child in question;
- placing the child in question in a mainstream school would be likely to be seriously disruptive to the educational well being of the other pupils at that school; or
- placing the child in question in a mainstream school would incur unreasonable levels of public expenditure that would not otherwise be incurred.

However, these exceptions should only occur in truly exceptional circumstances. Increasingly, children with additional support needs are educated in mainstream schools, or in special schools or units located within the campus of a mainstream school.

Making a placing request

Education authorities must have guidelines for allocating places in schools if there are more placing requests than there are places available. The education authority must let a parent have a copy of these guidelines on request.

Parents can make a placing request at any time, and at any stage of their children's education. Most placing requests are made when a child is starting primary school or is transferring to secondary. Parents may make as many placing requests as they like and name as many schools as they want, but the education authority only need to consider the first school named in any request. In the case of older pupils, it is the young person themselves who makes any placing request.

Placing requests must be made in writing. Most education authorities have a standard form which they prefer to use. Parents do not have to give reasons why they want their children to be placed in a particular school, unless the child or young person has additional support needs, in which case reasons are required. If the demand for places is high, then the more good reasons given, (i.e. reasons why the child should be given priority) the better the chances of success. In particular, the education authority must be careful to respect a choice of school based on the parents' religious or philosophical convictions (e.g. a Muslim parent may wish their daughter to attend a single sex school; or Roman Catholic parents may wish their children to attend a denominational school). If a child falls within one of the higher priority cases for placing in high demand schools, this should be mentioned. If there is a particular reason why one school would be more suitable for a child's abilities or needs then this should be included too.

If a placing request is made for a particular school for the start of the next academic session and is made within the correct timescale, then a decision must be reached by 30 April. For children or young people with additional support needs the deadline is 15 March; for others, each local authority will set their own deadline. You may receive notification of this, but if you have not you should contact the education department to check. Otherwise, the parent must have a decision within 2 months of the date of application. If the parent has not received a decision within these time limits, the education authority is deemed to have refused the placing request.

When can the education authority refuse a placing request?

If a placing request is made, the education authority must provide a place in the school specified, unless any of the following apply:

(a) Placing the child in the specified school would

   (i)   mean the education authority have to employ another teacher;

   (ii)   lead to significant expenditure on extending or altering the school accommodation or facilities;

   (iii)   be seriously detrimental to the child's continuity of education;

   (iv)   be likely to be seriously detrimental to order and discipline within the school;

   (v)   be likely to be seriously detrimental to the educational well-being of the pupils attending the school; or

   (vi)   make it necessary in future years for the authority to create an additional class or employ another teacher (primary schools only).

   (vii)   Though neither of the tests set out in paragraphs (i) and (ii) is satisfied, have the consequence that the capacity of the school would be exceeded in terms of pupil numbers,

(b) The education provided at that school is not suited to the age, ability or aptitude of the child;

(c) The child had previously been excluded from that school;

(d) The school is a special school, but the child does not have the additional support needs it caters for (this ground for refusal does not apply to children or young people with additional support needs);

(e) The school is a single sex school, and the child is not of the gender normally admitted there;

A placing request may also be refused if giving the child a place in the school would prevent the education authority keeping spaces there for children who may move into the area during the next year (these are called reserved places).

What if a placing request is refused?

Parents have a right of appeal against the refusal. An appeal must be lodged within 28 days of the refusal (or of the date the request was deemed to be refused). However, if the appeal requires to be made to the Additional Support Needs Tribunal, the time limit is two months (see **Appeals**).

One very important thing to bear in mind is that if a parent lodges an appeal against the refusal of a placing request, then they are not allowed to lodge another placing request appeal for the next 12 months. Parents should therefore think carefully before lodging a placing request appeal; it may be a good idea to discuss it fully with a solicitor who has experience of education law.

An appeal against a refusal of a placing request must be granted unless the education appeal committee, Sheriff or Tribunal is satisfied both that there is a ground for refusal and that it is appropriate for the placing request to be refused. Otherwise, the appeal must be allowed, and the pupil placed in the specified school.

Review of decisions

If a parent successfully appeals against the refusal of a placing request (whether at the appeal committee or the Sheriff court) then the education authority must review all of the cases of children whose placing requests for the same stage of education at the same school were also refused. It must then notify the parents in writing whether, on review, their child has now been granted a place at that school. These parents would then have 28 days from the date they received the review letter to lodge an appeal (provided they had not lodged an appeal within the previous 12 months).

This rule does not apply in the case of children or young people who have additional support needs.

See also

Additional Support for Learning
Appeals

Useful organisations

Enquire
Independent Special Education Advice (Scotland)
HM Inspectorate of Education
Parentzone

Useful publications:

Scottish Government (2007) *Choosing a School – a guide for parents* (available from the Scottish Government)

Legal references used in this book

Sections 28, 28A, 28B; Education (Scotland) Act 1980

Section 15; Standards in Scotland's Schools etc. Act 2000

Schedule 2; Education (Additional Support for Learning) (Scotland) Act 2004

CLASS SIZE AND STAFFING

Class sizes in Primary 1 to Primary 3

Regulations were introduced in 1999 with the aim of capping Primary 1 to Primary 3 classes (as from 1 August 2001) at thirty pupils during the course of "ordinary teaching sessions".

The (then) Scottish Executive published guidance in April 2007 that introduced a target class size for Primary 1 classes of 25. The "Concordat" between the Scottish Government and local authorities set a further target of reducing class sizes in P1 to P3 classes to a maximum of 18.

However, a recent decision by the Court of Session means that it is virtually impossible for local authorities to lawfully restrict class sizes in accordance with the targets or regulations where parents have made placing requests (and appeal their refusal).

Class sizes in primary and secondary schools

The maximum number of pupils for classes in primary and secondary schools are to be set following negotiation on a national basis in accordance with structures put in place under the McCrone Agreement on teachers pay and conditions.

The limits on class sizes are currently set as follows.

The maximum number of pupils should not normally be more than:

33 pupils in Primary 1 – 7 and Secondary 1 & 2;

30 pupils in Secondary 3 – 6 ; and

20 pupils in practical classes at secondary school (such as home economics, science, and technical classes).

Teachers may be asked to teach larger classes than these in certain circumstances (e.g. to cover for staff absences). They may not refuse to do so without good reason.

There are, however, *absolute* maximum limits which may not be exceeded and above which teachers may refuse to teach under any circumstances:

39 pupils in Primary 4 – 7 and Secondary 1 & 2; and

34 pupils in Secondary 3 & 4.

The education authority also has to make sure that there are not too many pupils in one classroom at a time, taking into consideration things like: the school building regulations, the space available, any equipment in the classroom, the type of classes taught there, and health and safety considerations. The education authority must keep a record of room sizes and the number of pupils they can hold, and you may ask to view this document – known as a "schedule of accommodation".

Composite classes

Pupils from different age groups in primary schools may sometimes be taught together in one "composite" class. Composite classes should be no larger than 25 pupils.

Official guidelines state that composite classes, where possible, should not:

• have pupils from more than two different age groups, which should be consecutive (i.e. P4/5, but not P4/5/6, nor P3/5);
• be set up just for convenience without first considering possible alternatives; nor
• be formed or regrouped after the school year has started (other than for educational reasons).

Special schools and units

The maximum class sizes for special schools and units are as follows.

Additional Support Needs arising from:	Number of pupils
Moderate learning difficulties	10
Profound learning difficulties	10
Severe physical impairment	8
Severe learning difficulties	8
Significant hearing impairment	6
Significant visual impairment	6
Language and communication difficulties	6
Social, emotional and behavioural difficulties	6

The maximum class size for children whose additional support needs arise from profound learning difficulties applies where teachers are complemented by support staff and education authorities are recommended to apply an adult/pupil ratio of 1:2.5.

Nursery Classes

Nursery classes should not exceed 20 children in size.

School staffing

The number of teaching staff is decided by the education authority, taking into account the numbers recommended by the Scottish Government.

Official guidance covers the basic number of teachers in any particular primary school. It is based on the number of pupils attending. The recommended number goes from:

• one teacher for schools with a roll of one to nineteen pupils, to

• up to 25 teachers for schools with a roll of 632 to 658.

In secondary schools, the staff numbers are worked out according to the number of pupils taking different courses and subjects there, the number of teaching periods, "non-teaching" time and other factors.

Additional funds to provide for extra teachers above the basic complement may be available to schools:

- which are difficult to run because of small or fluctuating pupil numbers;
- with a lot of pupils from socially-disadvantaged areas who may need extra tuition; or
- at which staff are away training or otherwise out of the classroom.

See also

Additional Support for Learning
School closures and changes

Useful organisations

Parentzone
Scottish Government

Legal references used in this section

East Lothian Council, Petitioners [2008] CSOH 137

Education (Lower Primary Class Sizes) (Scotland) Regulations 1999

Reg 8; Schools General (Scotland) Regulations 1975

Staff in School Education; STC/19 (Composite Class Guidelines)

Scottish Office Education Department Circular 14; December 1978, No. 1029

Part 2, Section 4 of the SNCT Handbook of Conditions of Service (SNCT, August 2007) www.snct.org.uk

CLOTHING AND SCHOOL UNIFORM

Clothing

What help with clothing should be available?

The law says that local authorities must provide any grants that they consider necessary to help with costs of clothing for pupils attending schools in their area. Each has its own scheme for clothing grants, and parents should contact their child's school for more information on the scheme operating in the local area.

The education authority must provide clothing (not necessarily free of charge) for any child whose inadequate or unsuitable clothes mean that he/she is unable to take full advantage of his/her education. It also has wide-ranging powers to provide clothing in a variety of circumstances. In practice, these powers are almost always exercised by way of a clothing grant scheme. However, the education authority must consider other requests made for clothing to be provided, even if the parents are not eligible under the scheme.

How much assistance is there?

The amount of the grant is decided by the education authority and will depend on income and other circumstances – most education authorities provide some financial assistance if the parents are in receipt of Income Support or other qualifying benefits. It is up to parents to apply for a clothing grant. The grant should cover some or all of the costs of any clothes and shoes required to enable their children to attend school, and any other special items of clothing required (e.g. PE kit) which are not provided by the school.

A clothing grant may be provided in cash but is more often provided by way of vouchers.

Do pupils have to wear school uniform?

Scots law is not specific on the question of school uniform. Nothing in the law says that pupils have to wear a school uniform. In practice, the rules about school uniform are left for the education authority or the school to decide. This can lead to considerable variation in the amount of freedom given to pupils on the types of clothes they can wear.

Schools almost always have rules or guidelines on the types of clothes allowed or preferred. This may include some common-sense rules which are imposed for health or safety reasons, for example:

- specialist sportswear may be required for certain activities (swimming caps, football boots etc.);
- loose clothing and dangling earrings may be forbidden in technical subjects using machinery or in PE where there may be a risk of injury.

Other rules on clothing or uniform may be to allow the school to promote a certain image or to improve the school ethos.

Written information on clothing and uniform must be made available to parents. Each school must provide information on its policy on clothing and uniform, including the approximate cost of each item of required uniform. The education authority must provide written information on its general policy on wearing school uniform. This is usually done through the school handbook.

Can a pupil be disciplined for not wearing school uniform?

A school may have school rules making school uniform compulsory, and pupils may legitimately be subject to discipline for a breach of those school rules. Such disciplinary measures should be reasonable and proportionate, and exclusion from school would be justified only in exceptional circumstances (or where parents were not allowing their child to wear school uniform).

What about human rights?

The European Commission of Human Rights has decided that it is not a breach of human rights to insist on school uniform being worn. This decision was based largely on the fact that the requirement only lasted during school hours, and therefore was not so serious as to constitute a breach of the Convention. More recently, court decisions in England and Wales have found that it was not a breach of human rights to restrict the wearing of particular clothing or jewellery, even where these were a manifestation of the pupil's religious beliefs.

Discrimination

School rules on uniform must not have a disproportionate effect on one gender, race or religion, nor involve a substantial disadvantage for children with disabilities. Rules that do are unlawful, unless justified on objective grounds. For example, the courts have decided that a ban on jewellery which effectively forbade the wearing of a Sikh "kara" bangle amounted to unlawful indirect discrimination on grounds of both race and religion.

See also

Disability discrimination
Discipline and punishment
Exclusion from school
Race discrimination
Religion or belief discrimination
Sex discrimination

Useful organisations

Citizens Advice Scotland
Equalities and Human Rights Commission
Parentzone

Legal references used in this section

Sections 11, 54, 55, 56; Education (Scotland) Act 1980

Shaw v. Strathclyde Regional Council 1988 SLT 313

Schedule 1, (2)(j); Education (School and Placing Information) (Scotland) Regulations 1982

Stevens v. UK, 3 March 1986; Application No. 11674/85

R. v. Chair and Governing Body of Cwmfelinfach Primary School (ex parte Roberts) [2001] EWHC Admin 242

Begum v. Denbigh High School [2006] UKHL 15

Playfoot v. Millais School [2007] EWHC 1698 (Admin)

X v.Y School [2007] EWHC 298 (Admin)

Singh v.Aberdare Girls' High School [2008] EWHC 1865 (Admin)

COMPLAINTS

What to do when something goes wrong

Parents and children are free to complain to various bodies or individuals when they are dissatisfied with something to do with their education. Parents should first try to get a problem or difficulty sorted out informally with the school. Most school handbooks have information for parents in on how to make a complaint. The steps below should help make sure that a problem or difficulty is presented in the right way to the right people.

Before making a complaint, parents should first consider:

Is the complaint justified? Is there reliable evidence to back up any claims made? Parents should make every effort to discover the full facts, and be cautious about airing unfounded complaints in public in case allegations of defamation (slander/libel) result.

Who is the best person to complain to? Often this will be the head teacher or another senior member of staff at the school concerned, but there may be circumstances in which it is appropriate to take a complaint to:

- the parent council or other parents' group;
- the education authority;
- the Director of Education or equivalent within the education authority;
- the local councillor or MSP;
- the Scottish Public Services Ombudsman (SPSO);
- the Scottish Ministers.

Certain official bodies also deal with complaints about:

- professional conduct of teachers – General Teaching Council for Scotland;
- Discrimination and Human Rights –Equality and Human Rights Commission.

Formal legal procedures also exist for hearing appeals from parents against a choice of school or exclusion from school, or matters relating to a Co-ordinated Support Plan (see **Appeals**). Some voluntary organisations may also be able to help parents with complaints, see **useful organisations** for further information.

Points to consider

How should a complaint be presented? The best way to start may be by talking to the people concerned, usually the head teacher or another senior staff member. It may be worthwhile confirming what was said in writing afterwards. Complaints should be put in writing if informal approaches have failed, and copies should be kept of all correspondence. Parents should be polite, but firm and insistent on getting an answer. Someone to represent a parent may be available, such as a friend, advice worker, representative from a parents' group, or (in some limited circumstances) a solicitor.

Complaints to the head teacher

It is advisable to take any complaints about a school to the head teacher or another member of staff to start with. If this is unsuccessful or the complaint is about the head teacher, a complaint to one of the other bodies mentioned below may be more appropriate. The head teacher may wish to make some enquiries into a complaint and parents should allow a reasonable time for this in waiting for any answer.

Complaints to the Parent Council or other parent body

Complaints about general matters, for example about a shortage of school textbooks or about courses taught at the school, may be worth taking to the Parent Council or PTA, if the school has one. These bodies may be able to put some pressure on the school or education authority to see what can be done. Complaints about policy matters can be drawn to the attention of national parents' organisations which may be interested in bringing these to the attention of central or local government. Some such bodies are listed at the end of the book.

Complaints to the education authority

Complaints which the school is unable or unwilling to deal with satisfactorily, should be addressed to the Director of Education or senior education officer. The education authority may have to make enquiries of its own, so it may be some time before a detailed answer is received. Complaints about the head teacher should be made to the Director of Education or equivalent within the education authority.

Additional support needs

Where a complaint is in relation to a pupil's additional support needs, the parent or young person may be able to access mediation or dispute resolution (see **Mediation** and **Dispute resolution**)

Complaints to elected representatives

Parents may write to or arrange to see their local councillor or MSP to take up a complaint about a school or education authority in general. The best time to do this is probably where a complaint to the school or education authority has not led to a satisfactory outcome. An elected representative is not legally obliged to deal with any complaint, but it is likely that he or she will agree to make enquiries on behalf of parents.

Complaints to the Scottish Ministers

Parents can make a complaint to the Scottish Ministers if they think an education authority has failed to carry out its educational duties. Parents should take advice before doing so.

The Scottish Ministers can conduct enquiries into such a complaint, but do not have to do so. They must give the education authority the opportunity to reply to a complaint.

Following investigation, if satisfied that the authority is at fault, the Scottish Ministers can order the authority to carry out its duties or take whatever measures are considered necessary to remedy the breach of duty. If the authority fails to act within the time limit given, the matter may be referred to the Court of Session, or the Scottish Ministers may arrange to perform the duty themselves and recoup the costs.

The Scottish Ministers can also issue general or specific directions to education authorities in matters relating to additional support needs and the authority or authorities concerned must comply with such a direction.

Complaints to the Scottish Public Services Ombudsman

Parents may complain to the Public Services Ombudsman if they believe the education authority has been guilty of "maladministration" or "service failure". The Ombudsman will, if necessary, look into a complaint and issue a report saying whether or not there has been "maladministration" or a "service failure" and, if so, what should be done. Although these recommendations are not legally binding, in the great majority of cases authorities accept and act upon the findings.

Maladministration may occur where:

- a rule has been unfairly or inefficiently applied or where the rule itself has caused the problem and could be improved;
- procedures have not been correctly followed;
- unreasonable delay or inefficiency has occurred in dealing with something;
- misleading or incorrect advice or information has been given, whether verbally or in writing;
- there has been a failure to keep somebody properly informed about a decision or proposal; or
- somebody has been treated with lack of proper consideration or respect.

A service failure may occur where there has been:

(a) a failure in a service provided by the authority, or

(b) a failure of the authority to provide a service which it was a function of the authority to provide.

The Ombudsman cannot investigate any action concerning the giving of instruction, whether secular or religious, or conduct, curriculum or discipline, in any educational establishment under the management of an education authority.

Parents must make sure that they have already used the education authority's own complaints procedures first, otherwise the Ombudsman cannot take up any complaint (unless it would be unreasonable to expect the parent to have used the authority's complaints procedures).

A copy of the Ombudsman's report is issued to the person who made the complaint and copies must be available at the authority's offices for any member of the public to look at.

See also

Additional Support for Learning
Advice and assistance
Appeals
Dispute Resolution
Education Authorities
Legal action
Mediation
Parental Involvement and Representation

Useful organisations

Additional Support Needs Tribunals
Citizens Advice Scotland
Enquire
Equalities and Human Rights Commission
General Teaching Council for Scotland
Independent Special Education Advice (Scotland)
Scottish Government
Scottish Public Services Ombudsman

Useful publications

Scottish Consumer Council (2006) *Complaints in Education* SCC: Glasgow (available through Consumer Focus Scotland)

Legal references used in this section

Sections 10, 11; Teaching Council (Scotland) Act 1965

Section 70; Education (Scotland) Act 1980

Scottish Public Services Ombudsman Act 2002

CONSULTING CHILDREN

Scots law views children as individuals with rights, and this is complemented by legal obligations to consult children and seek their views. However, while there is generally an obligation to *have regard* to the views of children, there is usually no absolute obligation to follow those views. Generally speaking, the requirement to seek a child's views depends on the age and level of maturity of the individual child, although a child of 12 is presumed to be of sufficient age and maturity to form a view on matters. Children under 12 may be of sufficient age and maturity to form a view, but this will depend on the individual child and the complexity of the matter in hand.

Parents

Parents are required by law to seek their child's views (and to have regard to those views) when making any major decision involving the fulfilment of parental responsibilities or the exercise of parental rights. Decisions about a child's education, such as the choice of school, or subject choices are examples of the types of decisions where parents should seek and take into account their children's views.

Local authorities

The level of the local authority's duty to consult children depends to an extent on whether the child is "looked after" by it. (A child is "looked after" if he or she is accommodated by the local authority, whether on a compulsory or voluntary basis, or if he or she is subject to a supervision requirement issued by a children's hearing or child protection order by a sheriff court).

The education authority has a duty to make sure the education provided to each pupil is directed towards the development of the individual pupil's talents and abilities. When deciding how best to fulfil this duty, the education authority has a duty to have regard to the views of the pupil (if the pupil wishes to express views) in relation to decisions that will significantly affect the pupil's education. This may be particularly relevant where the education authority is considering whether to educate a child outwith mainstream schooling, or is making decisions about the range of subjects offered in a particular school.

There is a duty on education authorities to issue an "annual statement of education improvement objectives" setting out their objectives for improving standards in school education in their areas. The education authority must give children in its area an opportunity to give their views on what the statement should include (see **Education authorities**).

Each school must also issue an annual "school development plan" setting out how it plans to improve the quality of education within the school. The pupils attending the school must be given the opportunity to make their views known on what should be in the development plan. The development plan must set out to what extent and how the pupils will be involved in the day to day running of the school. Some schools may have a pupil council or similar body to facilitate this process.

If a child is "looked after" by the local authority, then the local authority must seek (and have regard to) their views when making *any* decision about the child (compare this with the parent's duty to consult only when it is a *major* decision, or the education authority's duties in relation to *significant decisions*).

Children's hearings

When making any decision, children's hearings must give a child an opportunity to express their views and have regard to these views. The child's views on education may be particularly relevant where they are considering moving him or her to a foster home which may lead to a change of school, or are considering a requirement that he or she should stay at a residential school.

Accessibility strategies

In preparing their accessibility strategies, each education authority, or grant-aided or independent school must consult such children, parents and young persons as they think fit.

Additional support needs

There are specific provisions for seeking children's views in relation to their additional support needs (see **Additional Support for Learning**).

Additional Support Needs Tribunals for Scotland

Although the right to make a reference to a Tribunal belongs to the parent, the child in question has a right to attend the Tribunal hearing, unless the Tribunal considers that the welfare or interests of that child would be prejudiced by being present.

Children can give evidence at the Tribunal. However children under 12 years of age may only do so if the Tribunal considers that the evidence of the child is necessary to enable a fair and just hearing of the reference; and that the welfare and interests of the child will not be prejudiced.

If the Tribunal allows a child aged 11 or less to give evidence in person, it may appoint someone to help the child to give evidence. That person will be paid for by the Tribunal.

Courts

In relation to education matters, courts are only specifically required to take into account a child's views when they are deciding whether to substitute their decision for that of the children's hearing in the event of a successful appeal. However, if a child gives evidence in a court case concerned with the child's own education, or if their views are otherwise made known to the Tribunal, the court is likely to regard that evidence as relevant.

See also

Accessibility strategies
Additional Support for Learning

Children's hearings
Looked after children
Overview - children's rights

Useful organisations

Article 12
Children in Scotland
Scotland's Commissioner for Children and Young People

Useful publications

Children in Scotland (2003) *Consulting with children and young people on accessibility strategies: A good practice guide*

Scottish Consumer Council (2008) *School Councils and Pupil Participation in Scottish Schools* (available from Consumer Focus Scotland)

Legal references used in this section

Sections 2, 5, 6; Standards in Scotland's Schools etc (Scotland) Act 2000

Section 6; Children (Scotland) Act 1995

Section 3; Education (Disability Strategies and Pupils' Educational Records) (Scotland) Act 2002

Rules 27, 33; Additional Support Needs Tribunals for Scotland (Practice and Procedure) Rules 2006

CONSULTING PARENTS

Parents have a right to be consulted by the education authority before it goes ahead with certain decisions about educational provision in its area. See **School closures and changes**.

The Standards in Scotland's Schools etc. (Scotland) Act 2000 includes many provisions to make sure that parents are consulted on key issues at both school and education authority level.

Annual statement of education improvement objectives

The education authority must consult with parents' groups (among others) in preparing its annual statement of education improvement objectives. The statement must include details of how the education authority will try to involve parents in promoting the education of their children (see **Education authorities**).

School Development Plan

Each year the education authority must prepare, for each of its schools, a school development plan. The development plan sets objectives for each school based on the annual statement of education improvement objectives. The development plan must be prepared after consultation with (among others) the Parent Council, and any other parents' groups for that school. Again an annual report must be prepared to show what has been done to put the plan into practice within the school.

Parents of pupils at the school are entitled to free access to the plan and the report on request (and to a free copy of their summaries).

Review of school performance

The education authority must, from time to time, assess the quality of each school's education against its own measures and standards for judging performance. Where a school fails to meet the standards, the education authority must take action to put right the problem(s).

When deciding the measures and standards of performance, the education authority must consult with parents' groups (among others). The measures and standards must be published.

Sex education

Although there is no statutory requirement to consult in relation to sex education, Scottish Government guidance states that schools should consult parents and carers when developing their sex education programmes, and parents and carers should have the opportunity to examine the materials which will be used, in advance.

Accessibility Strategies

In preparing their accessibility strategies, each education authority, or grant-aided or independent school must consult such children, parents and young persons as they think fit.

Additional support needs

There are specific provisions for seeking parent's views in relation to their children's additional support needs (see **Additional Support for Learning**).

See also

Accessibility strategies
Additional Support for Learning
Parent-teacher and parents' associations
Information for parents
Legal action
Parental involvement and representation
School closures and changes

Useful organisations

Enquire
Parentzone
Scottish Parent Council Association
Scottish Parent Teacher Council

Useful publications

Scottish Executive (2006) *Parents as Partners in their Children's Learning: Toolkit* (available from the Scottish Government)

Legal references used in this section

Education (Publication and Consultation etc) (Scotland) Regulations 1981

Sections 4 to 7; Standards in Scotland's Schools etc. (Scotland) Act 2000

Scottish Executive Circular 2/2001, issued in terms of section 56 of the Standards in Scotland's Schools etc. (Scotland) Act 2000

Harvey v. Strathclyde Regional Council 1989 SLT 612

Section 3; Education (Disability Strategies and Pupils' Educational Records) (Scotland) Act 2002

CO-ORDINATED SUPPORT PLANS

Co-ordinated Support Plan

The majority of children and young people with additional support needs will not receive any statutory documentation in relation to those needs.

However, some children and young people require a Co-ordinated Support Plan (or CSP). A child or young person requires a Co-ordinated Support Plan if they fulfil all of the following criteria:

• they must have additional support needs;

• those needs must be likely to continue for more than a year;

• those needs must have or be likely to have a significant adverse effect on the school education of the child or young person; and

• those needs require significant additional support by the education authority and by at least one other "appropriate agency" or authority function.

Additional support needs may have a significant adverse effect on a child or young person's school education whether they arise from a single factor ("a complex factor") or a number of factors in combination ("multiple factors").

Appropriate agencies include: a different local authority; a Health Board; Careers Scotland or further and higher education institutions. Another authority function is most likely to involve the authority's social work functions.

Where the child or young person is educated by the education authority the authority must establish whether or not the child or young person requires a co-ordinated support plan if:

- they are requested to do so by the parent or young person and that request is not an unreasonable one; or
- a child or young person comes to their attention as having additional support needs and requiring or appearing to require a co-ordinated support plan.

If an education authority establishes that a child or young person requires a co-ordinated support plan, then they have a duty to prepare one for him or her.

A Co-ordinated Support Plan includes:

- a statement of the education authority's conclusions as to:
  - the factor(s) giving rise to the child or young person's additional support needs;
  - taking into account these factors, the educational goals set;
  - the additional support required in order to achieve those goals; and
  - the persons who will provide that support (this may include other agencies);
- a nomination of a school the child or young person should attend;
- the name and contact details of:
  - the individual (from the education authority or delegated by them) who is responsible for co-ordinating the provision of additional support for the child or young person between the various agencies concerned; and
- the name and contact details of:
  - an officer of the education authority from whom the parent or young person (as the case may be) can obtain further information and advice.

The plan will also contain the following information:

- the name, address, contact telephone number, date of birth, gender, preferred language or form of communication, school currently attended and the date of entry to that school of the child or young person;

- the name, address, contact telephone number, relationship to the child or young person and preferred language or form of communication of each parent of the child or young person;
- a profile of the skills and capabilities of, and any other relevant information relating to the child or young person;
- any views expressed by the child / young person / parent(s) on the plan; and
- the review timetable for the plan in accordance with the statutory time limits.

The educational goals referred to above should be chosen with a view to helping the child or young person develop their personality, talents and mental and physical abilities to their fullest potential.

Where an education authority has prepared a co-ordinated support plan, they must provide additional support for the child or young person in accordance with the contents of the plan (insofar as they have the power to do so). The authority must also seek to ensure that other agencies named in the plan provide the additional support allocated to them to provide in the plan. There are statutory powers contained in the Additional Support for Learning Act 2004 which allow an education authority to make an official request for help in providing for the additional support needs of a child or young person.

Time Limits

Where a parent (or young person) makes a written request that the authority determine whether or not a child (or young person) requires a Co-ordinated Support Plan, the authority must notify the parent (or young person) as to whether or not they propose to comply with that request no later than 4 weeks after the request is received.

Where the authority has decided (whether following a parental request or otherwise) that it will determine whether or not a child or young person requires a CSP, it must formally inform the parent of their proposal to do so. Then, within 16 weeks of that date (i.e. the date of informing the parent(s) or young person) the authority must:

- give a copy of the completed plan to the parent(s) or young person; or
- inform the parent(s) or young person as to the reasons for their decision that the child or young person does not require a plan.

The Code of Practice indicates that the authority should aim to let the parent or young person know whether the child or young person requires a CSP or not within the first 4 weeks of that 16 week period.

The 16 week time limit need not be adhered to if it is impractical to do so due to one of a number of exceptions, including:

- the parent or young person wish to provide additional advice and information after the time limit for doing so;
- the parent or young person has made an assessment request which cannot be completed within the time limit;
- the authority has requested advice, information or help from another agency and that agency has not complied within the time limit;
- exceptional personal circumstances affecting the child / parent / young person;
- the child / parent / young person is absent from the area for 4 weeks or more; or
- the child or young person fails to keep an appointment for an examination or assessment.

If it becomes clear to the authority that they will not be able to meet the 16 week time limit, the authority must inform the parent or young person of that fact, the reasons for the delay and the new date on which a plan will be provided (or the reasons why a plan is not required). In any event the maximum period cannot be extended beyond 24 weeks.

Reviews

The education authority has a general duty to keep under consideration the adequacy of all Co-ordinated Support Plans for children and young people in their area. It must carry out a review of each plan one year after it has been prepared, and thereafter one year after the last review was completed. Reviews can be carried out more frequently than that on request from the parent or young person or when the education authority considers it necessary or expedient to do so due to a change of circumstances.

On request from the parent or young person, the education authority must carry out a review, unless it considers that request to be unreasonable.

The review process should last no longer than 12 weeks, although the time limit may be extended in the circumstances as described above for the initial CSP process – to an absolute maximum of 20 weeks.

In carrying out a review the education authority must establish whether the child or young person still requires a Co-ordinated Support Plan. If the authority establish that the child or young person still requires a Co-ordinated Support Plan, then the plan must be continued and the authority will make such amendments as they consider necessary or appropriate. If the authority establish that the child or young person no longer requires a plan, then it will be discontinued.

See Also

Additional Support for Learning
Appeals

Useful organisations

Additional Support Needs Tribunals
Enquire
Independent Special Education Advice (Scotland)
Parentzone

Useful publications

Enquire Factsheet 15: *Co-ordinated support plans (CSPs)*

Legal references used in this section

Sections 2, 9, 10, 11; Education (Additional Support for Learning) (Scotland) Act 2004

Additional Support for Learning (Co-ordinated Support Plan) (Scotland) Amendment Regulations 2005

CURRICULUM (what is taught)

"Curriculum" is the word used to describe what is taught to children at school. It refers to the full range of subjects that are studied at a school.

What is taught at school

By law there are only two subjects which must be taught by schools:

• Religious education ("religious instruction"); and
• Gaelic in Gaelic speaking areas.

Beyond this, the Scottish Government, through Learning and Teaching Scotland, issues guidelines on the curriculum, which are followed to a greater or lesser extent by education authorities. The education authority has a duty to provide pupils with an adequate and efficient education suitable to his or her age, aptitude and ability. School education must also be directed to the development of the personality, talents and mental and physical abilities of each child or young person to their fullest potential. The education authority and head teachers share responsibility for the management and delivery of the curriculum in schools. In the case of independent schools, it is the proprietor (usually the school governors or directors) and the head teacher.

The 5 to 14 curriculum

These guidelines (published by Learning and Teaching Scotland) cover primary school education and the first stages of secondary school education. The guidelines try to make sure that the curriculum is:

- Broad: covering a wide range of subject areas;
- Balanced: giving due attention to each area;
- Coherent: building on what pupils have already learned; and
- Progressive: providing challenging but attainable targets for all pupils.

The 5 to 14 curriculum lists six curriculum areas which should be taught:

- Language: reading, writing, discussion, possibly Gaelic or other languages;
- Mathematics: number, shape, etc.;
- Expressive arts: art, craft, music, physical education, drama;
- Environmental studies: geography, history, nature study, science etc.;
- Religious and moral education; and
- Personal and social development and Health education.

There are also cross-curricular aspects which address common themes across different subject areas. They cover core aspects of pupils' learning. There is a strong emphasis on social inclusion. The five aspects are:

- Enterprise in Education;
- Education for citizenship;
- Financial Education;
- Education for Sustainable Development;
- Information and Communications Technology.

Assessment

Subject areas are assessed at six levels, starting at level A and working through to level E which many pupils will attain by second year of secondary school. Level F is also available to continue to challenge pupils who may reach level E before then. Pupils are allowed to progress through the levels at their own pace, being regularly assessed by their teacher. For Maths and English, there are national tests to assess the level of attainment.

Beyond 5 to 14

Beyond the 5 to 14 age range many teachers will determine the curriculum through the use of past examinations on their subjects and information provided by the Scottish Qualifications Authority. It is expected that most pupils will take courses leading to the award of Standard Grades and / or other certificates.

Curriculum for Excellence

Schools in Scotland are currently in the process of changing from the 5 to 14 curriculum to new guidelines, known as "A Curriculum for Excellence". The Scottish Government intends to phase in the Curriculum for Excellence from 2009/10.

Under "A Curriculum for Excellence", the purposes of education are described. They are to enable all young people to become:

• successful learners;
• confident individuals;
• responsible citizens; and
• effective contributors.

These are described as the four capacities.

In addition, there are seven principles for curriculum design:

• challenge and enjoyment;
• breadth;
• progression;
• depth;
• personalisation and choice;
• coherence; and
• relevance.

Curriculum for Excellence aims to simplify the curriculum, encourage more learning through experiences (or "active learning"), and create a single framework for the curriculum and assessment for pupils aged 3-18.

Curriculum for Excellence will not be a static document, but will involve a continuous process of review to make sure that the curriculum remains up to date. It aims to be more flexible, offering a framework within which schools and teachers can work.

There are eight curriculum areas:

- Sciences;
- Languages;
- Mathematics;
- Expressive arts;
- Social studies;
- Technologies;
- Health and wellbeing; and
- Religious and moral education.

In each of these areas, there are now draft experiences and outcomes, which can be downloaded from the Learning and Teaching Scotland website.

See also

Additional Support for Learning
Gaelic
Examinations and assessment
Religious education and observance

Useful organisations

Learning and Teaching Scotland
Parentzone

Useful publications

Scottish Executive (2004) *A Curriculum for Excellence: The Curriculum Review Group* (available from the Scottish Government)

Scottish Executive (2004) *Homework: A guide for parents* (available from the Scottish Government)

Scottish Executive (2005) Making the Difference: Personal Learning Planning Practice Advice for Parents (available from the Scottish Government)

Legal references used in this section

Sections 1, 8; Education (Scotland) Act 1980

Section 2(1); Standards in Scotland's Schools etc. (Scotland) Act 2000

Guidance on Flexibility in the Curriculum SEED Circular 3/2001

DENOMINATIONAL SCHOOLS

Many pupils in Scotland go to schools which are associated with a religious denomination. Most are Roman Catholic schools, managed by the education authority, though there is one Jewish school and several Episcopalian schools. Although primarily intended for children of parents belonging to the denomination in question, they must also be open to other children. Any church or other religious body can ask the education authority to open a denominational school. The education authority does not have to do this, although it may decide to if there is likely to be sufficient demand. Religious bodies can also establish their own, independent schools.

Parents have a right to ensure that their children are educated in accordance with their own religious or philosophical convictions. This right does not mean that parents can insist on a school being provided, or on a place for their child at a denominational school. However, the education authority must take account of parental convictions when deciding things like placing requests.

Management of denominational schools

Denominational schools are subject to all the same legal requirements as other education authority schools. Even the rules for religious education and observance are the same. There are also additional rules which apply only to denominational schools. At a denominational school:

- teachers appointed must have their religious beliefs and character approved by the religious body;
- the amount of religious education and observance cannot be less than is customary for schools of that type;

- the school must allow for religious examinations to be held; and

- an unpaid supervisor of religious instruction (e.g. a priest, rabbi or imam) approved by the religious body must report to the education authority on the efficiency of religious education provided – the supervisor may attend the school any time religious instruction is to be provided.

Complaints about whether the school is complying with these obligations may be dealt with by the Scottish Ministers, if they are asked to look into the matter. The education authority remains responsible for deciding on the curriculum (what is to be taught) at denominational schools, in consultation with the religious body.

Attendance

A child cannot be refused admission to any education authority school on the grounds of the child's or parents' religious affiliations. Nor can a religious body insist that a child attend a certain school. It is probably lawful for an education authority to give higher priority in ranking placing requests to pupils whose parents have an affiliation to the relevant denomination. Independent schools are permitted to restrict intake based on religious affiliation.

Religious education and observance

The rules are exactly the same as for other schools, including the parental right to withdraw their children from religious education or observance. If a child is a boarder, he or she has the right to be allowed time outside school hours to practice their parent's religion, even if this is different from the school's.

See also

Religion and belief discrimination
Religious education and observance

Useful organisations

General Teaching Council for Scotland
Scottish Catholic Education Service

Legal references used in this section

Article 2, Protocol 1, Schedule 1 of the Human Rights Act 1998

Sections 9, 10, 21; Education (Scotland) Act 1980

DEVOLVED SCHOOL MANAGEMENT

In law, it is the education authority (rather than the school itself) that has legal duties towards pupils. Many of the day-to-day tasks and responsibilities are carried out by head teachers and senior management teams of schools, as employees of the education authority. Education authorities must have a scheme for delegating responsibility for preparing school development plans to the head teachers of each school. This scheme can (but does not have to) delegate other management responsibilities to the head teacher. This puts the practice of "devolved school management" on a statutory footing.

The thinking behind devolved school management is to give to those who know the school best more involvement in, and responsibility for, making decisions.

Schools are given a budget to cover, for example, salaries, costs of books and other teaching materials, costs of furniture, fixtures and fittings, and costs of other supplies and services. The head teacher then decides how to allocate the school's budget. Parents do not have to be formally consulted. However, if parents feel additional expenditure is needed in a particular area, then they are free to raise this with the head teacher. If parents remain unhappy with the way the school budget is being spent, then they can raise this with the parent council or the education authority.

Under a scheme of devolved school management, head teachers can also be given increased responsibility for staff recruitment.

See also

Parental Involvement and Representation

Legal references used in this section

Section 8 of the Standards in Scotland's Schools etc. (Scotland) Act 2000

DISABILITY DISCRIMINATION

It is unlawful to discriminate against disabled pupils at school on the grounds of their disability.

In relation to education the law applies to all schools, not just education authority schools, though the body responsible for it differs:

- in public schools (including pre-school education provision, primary school and secondary school) the education authority is the responsible body;
- in independent or grant aided schools, the managers are the responsible body.

A pupil is disabled if they have a physical or mental impairment which has a substantial and long term adverse effect on his or her ability to carry out normal day-to-day activities.

An effect on a pupil's normal day-to-day activities is "substantial" if it is more than minor or trivial and it is "long term" if it has lasted for or is likely to last for at least 12 months.

"Physical or mental impairment" includes sensory impairments (such as hearing or sight impairments). Hidden impairments are also covered: for example, mental illness (provided they are clinically well-recognised), learning disabilities and conditions such as epilepsy or Crohn's disease.

An impairment is said to affect normal day-to-day activities if it affects one or more of the following:

- mobility;
- manual dexterity;
- physical co-ordination;
- continence;

- ability to lift, carry or otherwise move everyday objects;
- speech, hearing or eyesight;
- memory or ability to concentrate, learn or understand; or
- perception of the risk of physical danger.

The following conditions are automatically taken to be a disability: cancer; HIV infection; multiple sclerosis; a long-term severe disfigurement; and a visual impairment (where the person is registered or certified as blind or partially sighted).

What constitutes disability discrimination?

It is unlawful for a school or education authority to discriminate against a disabled pupil or prospective pupil:

- in relation to admissions policy or practice;
- in the education or associated services provided or offered by the school or education authority; or
- by excluding them from school (either permanently or temporarily).

Disability discrimination may occur in two ways:

- by treating a disabled pupil less favourably for a reason related to their disability, without justification; or
- by failing, without justification, to take reasonable steps to avoid placing disabled pupils at a substantial disadvantage compared with non-disabled pupils.

For example, it would be disability discrimination to refuse someone a place at a school simply because they were disabled (unless the refusal could be justified). It may be disability discrimination where a school refuses to take reasonable steps to assist disabled pupils. A disabled pupil may require extra time to complete tasks or careful planning with regard to curriculum delivery or dietary considerations. (see **Accessibility strategies**)

However, there are some circumstances where a school are not required to take "reasonable steps". There is no duty to provide auxiliary aids and services or to remove or alter physical features of a school, though this is likely to come under the general provisions of the Education (Additional Support for Learning) Act 2004 (see **Additional Support for Learning**).

Where there has been disability discrimination in the delivery of education, a disabled pupil (or a parent acting as their legal representative) can seek conciliation, and/or raise legal action in the Sheriff court. Specialist legal advice should be sought from the Equality and Human Rights Commission or a solicitor. There is no financial compensation available for disability discrimination in schools.

See also

Accessibility strategies
Equal opportunities and equality strategies

Useful organisations

Capability Scotland
Enquire
Equalities and Human Rights Commission
Independent Special Education Advice (Scotland)
Parentzone

Useful publications

Children in Scotland (2007) *Access All Areas: What children and young people think about accessibility, inclusion and additional support at school*

Disability Rights Commission (undated) *Code of Practice for Schools* (available from the Equalities and Human Rights Commission)

Legal references used in this section

Sections 1, 28A-28N; Disability Discrimination Act 1995, as amended by Special Educational Needs and Disability Act 2001 and by Disability Discrimination Act 2005

Disability Discrimination (Blind and Partially Sighted Persons) Regulations 2003

DISCIPLINE AND PUNISHMENT

Schools, in educating pupils, may impose disciplinary sanctions where necessary. Education authorities have a duty to promote reasonable and responsible social attitudes and relationships, consideration for others, good manners, good attitudes to work, initiative and self-reliance among their pupils. Schools have duties not to allow serious disruption to the educational well being of their pupils. They have duties relating to the safety and supervision of their pupils as well as duties (as employers) to their staff. There is therefore a legitimate interest in maintaining good order and asking parents and pupils to comply with school rules. Disciplinary sanctions are one way in which these duties may be achieved.

The Scottish courts have upheld this principle, confirming that parents have a responsibility to ensure (as best they can) that their children obey school rules. Discipline at school should be seen as a shared responsibility between school, parents and pupils.

Disciplinary measures should not be unreasonable, should not be excessive, and should be in line with any policy, guidelines or procedures laid down by the school or education authority. The policies on discipline should be available to parents.

Detention

It has been argued that detention of children outwith school hours would be unlawful without parental consent. This is likely to be the case, but has not been considered by the courts. Detention within school hours (e.g. at lunch time) is lawful where reasonably and necessarily carried out for educational or disciplinary reasons.

Human Rights

In human rights law, the imposition of disciplinary penalties is seen as an integral part of schooling. This is subject to certain restrictions:

- disciplinary sanctions must not amount to inhuman or degrading treatment;
- disciplinary sanctions must not conflict with the parents' right to ensure that their children are educated in accordance with their own religious or philosophical convictions;
- disciplinary sanctions must not be applied in a discriminatory way.

Discipline

The school must make sure that any punishment does not amount to unlawful discrimination: for example it should not be more difficult to comply with disciplinary rules for one race, gender or other group. Otherwise, this may amount to unlawful indirect discrimination.

Corporal punishment

The use of corporal (i.e. physical) punishment is no longer permitted in Scottish schools, either education authority or independent schools. The defence of "reasonable chastisement" is no longer open to teachers and the use of force as punishment is now likely to be treated as a criminal assault as well as grounds for a civil action seeking damages.

See also

Equal opportunities and equality duties
Legal action
Safety and supervision
School rules

Useful organisations

Equalities and Human Rights Commission
Parentzone

Useful publications

Scottish Executive (2001) *Better Behaviour Better Learning: Report of the Discipline Task Group* (available from the Scottish Government)

Legal references used in this section

Wyatt v. Wilson 1994 SLT 1135

Reg 11 of the Schools General (Scotland) Regulations 1975

Section 48A; Education (Scotland) Act 1980;

Section 16; Standards in Scotland's Schools etc. (Scotland) Act 2000

Sched I, (2)(k) & (3)(w); Education (School and Placing Information) (Scotland) Regulations 1982

Articles 3, 5, 13, Prot 1, Art 2; Human Rights Act 1998

Campbell and Cosans v. United Kingdom (1982) 4 EHRR 293

Warwick v. United Kingdom (1986) 60 DR 5

DISPUTE RESOLUTION

Disputes relating to a child's or young person's additional support needs (see **Additional Support for Learning**) may be referred to a process of independent adjudication, which is referred to in the legislation simply as "dispute resolution".

The parent or young person may make an application for independent adjudication in relation to a dispute about any of the following:

- a decision by the education authority that a child or young person has (or does not have) additional support needs;

- a decision by the education authority as to the type of additional support needs a child or young person has;

- a refusal by the education authority to determine whether or not a child or young person has additional support needs;

- a refusal by the education authority of an assessment request made by a parent or young person;

- a decision by the education authority as to how, or by whom, an assessment or examination should be carried out.

- a failure by the education authority to provide the additional support (whether relating to education or not) required by the child or young person;

- a failure by the education authority to make a statutory request for help from another appropriate agency (e.g. the Health Board) in relation to a child's or young person's additional support needs.

The application is made, in the first instance, in writing to the education authority. The authority's policy on additional support needs should indicate to whom such applications ought to be addressed.

There is no formal time limit for making an application to the authority, although the education authority need only accept an application if it is reasonable. A referral made a long time after the incident or failure complained of may not be a reasonable one. Similarly, a referral may not be reasonable if the parent has not raised the issue of a matter of concern before.

The application by the parent or young person must include the following information:

• the name and address of the parent or young person making the application and (if different) of the child or young person the application is about;

• the subject matter of the application (from the list above) and a summary of the background circumstances giving rise to the application;

• a copy of any advice, information, requests or decisions which the applicant wishes to be taken into account (e.g. copies of minutes, medical reports or letters, other information);

• the grounds for the application (with references to the relevant parts of the Act);

• the applicant's views on how the dispute should be resolved; and

• if known, the views of the child or young person on the application.

Many authorities will have a standard form for dispute resolution which includes sections for all of the above information.

The application is made, in the first place, to the education authority. Within ten working days (assuming the application is valid) the education authority must provide confirmation of the acceptance of the application and, at the same time, send a request to the Scottish Ministers to nominate an independent adjudicator. The education authority must then appoint the nominated adjudicator (and meet his or her fees for the adjudication).

Within ten working days of the acceptance of the application, the authority must provide a copy of its own written submissions to the applicant (and, where appropriate, the child or young person as well) which will include:

- the authority's views on the circumstances giving rise to the application;
- the authority's views on the application itself and any supporting material provided with it;
- a copy of any further advice, information, requests or decisions which the applicant wishes to be taken into account; and
- the authority's views on how the dispute should be resolved.
- Within twenty-five working days of the acceptance of the application, the education authority must send the application, its response and any further observations made by either side (further observations are allowed during the ten working days following the authority's response) to the independent adjudicator.

The adjudicator will then review the case and, in doing so, must have regard to:

- the application;
- the authority's response;
- any further observations made by either side; and
- any further information or advice requested by the adjudicator.
- Within a period of fifteen working days, the adjudicator must report back to the authority as to his or her recommendations on how the dispute should be resolved. The education authority then has a further ten working days to issue its decision as to what course of action it will take in light of the recommendations. The decision must include details of:
- the facts on which the decision is based;
- the reasons for their decision;
- where applicable, the reasons for not following (in whole or in part) the recommendations of the adjudicator; and

• the authority's view on the effect of the decision on the child or young person.

See also

Additional Support for Learning
Complaints
Mediation

Useful organisations

Enquire
Independent Special Education Advice (Scotland)
Parentzone
Scottish Government

Useful publications

Enquire Factsheet 5: *Resolving Disagreements*

Legal references used in this section

Additional Support for Learning Dispute Resolution (Scotland) Regulations 2005

EDUCATION AUTHORITIES

There are 32 local authorities throughout Scotland. Local authorities have duties covering a whole host of public functions, including education. Each local authority consists of its elected members – councillors – and its employees who have the task of putting into practice the council's policies and carrying out its various duties. For the purposes of education legislation, each local authority is called an education authority.

Education committees

The education authority must set up an education committee, which deals with policy issues in relation to education. The committee will be made up of councillors, teachers, representatives of religious bodies and may also include parent or pupil representatives. The education committee may also set up sub-committees to deal with specific issues. The meetings of the education committee and sub-committees are ordinarily open to the public. Copies of the agendas for the meetings, reports to be considered and the minutes of previous meetings should also be available. There are specific matters which the education committee is entitled by law to keep confidential and it is allowed to refuse public access to meetings and reports under those circumstances.

The Director of Education

Each local authority will have a number of departments devoted to the different areas of work it is responsible for. One of these departments, headed by the Director of Education, will deal with the local authority's duties in relation to education. Increasingly local authorities are adopting non-traditional organisational structures where the Director of Education may be known as, for example, the Director of Children's Services, but will nonetheless carry out the same functions, along with other functions he or she may be responsible for.

What must education authorities do?

The law says that there are some things an education authority must do. For example:

- make sure there is "adequate and efficient" provision of school and pre-school education in its area;
- make sure the education provided to each child and young person at its schools is directed towards the development of the personality, talents and mental and physical abilities of that child to their fullest potential;
- provide for pupils' additional support needs;
- provide boarding accommodation where necessary;
- provide books, stationery, materials etc;
- consult with parents about school closures and other proposed changes;
- provide parents with information about schools;
- provide a psychological service;
- make sure pupils are adequately supervised;
- provide adequate facilities for social, cultural and recreational activities for school pupils;
- provide adequate facilities for physical education and training for school pupils.

If the law says an education authority has a duty to do something then it must carry out its duty. Except in certain specified circumstances, an education authority is not excused from performing a duty due to a lack of money. However, if there are a number of different ways of carrying out a duty, the authority may choose how to do so.

Annual Statement of Educational Improvement Objectives

Each year the education authority must prepare and publish a statement setting its objectives for improving education, in line with the current national priorities in education and performance indicators (as defined by the Scottish Ministers).

When preparing the statement it must consult with:

- groups that represent parents in the area;
- groups that represent teachers in the area; and
- people other than teachers employed within schools.

Children and young people should also have an opportunity to have their voices heard.

The annual statement must include details of:

- how the education authority will try to involve parents in promoting the education of their children;
- how the education authority will encourage equal opportunities; and
- how, and in what circumstances, the education authority will provide Gaelic medium education and develop its provision of such education.

A separate annual report on the success (or otherwise) of the education authority in meeting these objectives must also be prepared.

What other things can the education authority do?

Additionally, the law gives education authorities powers to do certain things. These are things the authority have a discretion to do (or not). Examples of an education authority's discretionary powers include:

- providing nursery education for children who are not entitled to it;
- providing school meals and milk at a charge for pupils not entitled to free school meals;
- authorising medical examination of pupils in the interests of cleanliness;
- providing school library facilities;
- establishing and maintaining swimming pools, sports centres, youth and community centres and clubs; etc.

The education authority's discretion is not totally without limitations as it must be exercised reasonably. Decisions of the authority may be subject to challenge by way of judicial review (see **Legal action** for explanation of judicial review).

Can the education authority do whatever it wants to?

If an education authority has neither a *duty* nor a *power* to do something, it is not allowed to do it. The education authority would be said to be acting *ultra vires* (outwith their powers). Pupils or parents may be able to take legal action to stop the authority from acting *ultra vires*.

However, under the Local Government in Scotland Act 2003, authorities have a general duty to advance well-being. It is hoped that this will enable authorities to be more responsive to the communities they serve. Guidance to the Act suggests that services for children and young people and access to education are key factors in improving well-being.

Complaints

If an education authority is not carrying out its legal duties or has done something it is not authorised to do, this can be addressed through the education authority's own internal complaints procedures. If that fails, a referral of the matter to the Scottish Ministers or to the Scottish Public Services Ombudsman may be considered. Parents may be able to raise an action in the courts, either in their own name or their child's.

See also

Complaints
Legal action

Useful organisations

Scottish Public Services Ombudsman

Legal references used in this section

Sections 70, 135; Education (Scotland) Act 1980

Local Government in Scotland Act 2003

Scottish Public Services Ombudsman Act 2002

EMPLOYMENT OF SCHOOLCHILDREN

There are a number of limitations on the times and hours worked and the type of work undertaken by schoolchildren. School children are only allowed to carry out "light work". Light work is work which does not jeopardise a child's safety, health, development, attendance at school or participation in work experience.

The legislation limits employment according to age:

• under the age of 10 children are not allowed to be employed at all;

• children aged 10 and over may be employed by their parents to do occasional light gardening or farming work;

• children aged 13 and over may be employed by to do light gardening or farming work. They may do a paper round, and may undertake light work in shops, hairdressers, offices, cafés, restaurants, stables or hotels;

• children aged 14 or over may undertake any light work which is not specifically excluded (for example, selling alcohol, working at heights, working with harmful chemicals or "adult material" etc.).

Children may not be employed in any industrial undertaking (including mines and quarries, manufacturing industry, construction and the transport of passengers or goods by road, rail or inland waterway), nor in a ship. However, children aged 14 or over may be employed in a training ship on a course recognised by the education authority.

There are also limits on the amount of time a child can be in employment:

- no child of school age is allowed to work before 7am or after 7pm on any day or for more than 2 hours on a school day or a Sunday. Nor may they work for more than one hour before school;
- children aged 14 or under may not work for more than 5 hours on Saturdays or school holidays, nor for more than 25 hours in a week;
- children aged 15 may not work for more than 8 hours on Saturdays or school holidays, nor for more than 35 hours in a week;
- children of school age are not allowed to work more than 4 hours in a day without having a break of at least one hour, and must have a period of at least 2 weeks a year when they are neither working nor at school.

An employer who breaks these restrictions can be prosecuted. Parents may be asked for information about their child's employment, and a deliberate failure to provide accurate information can lead to prosecution.

Many rules on the employment of schoolchildren are contained in local bye-laws for each area. Parents should check with the local authority what these are. It is important to remember that the rules on employment of school children cover both paid and unpaid work. Local bye-laws cover the restrictions on children being employed in street trading.

Once a child reaches school leaving age (16 years old), the above restrictions no longer apply, even if he or she is still attending school. There are restrictions in employment law on the type of work under 18's are allowed to do, and these will obviously apply until the young person is 18.

Public performances

Children can take part in public performances (e.g. stage, television, film) and rehearsals as long as a licence is granted by their education authority. No licence is needed for school or amateur productions.

During a child's final year of compulsory education he or she will normally undertake a period of work experience. This usually lasts for about a week, but can last longer by arrangement between the education authority and 'employer'. The legal limitations on the *time* or *hours* worked will not apply during this period of work experience, although the limitations on the *type* of work will still apply. A child will not be paid for the work he or she does during the work experience placement, although additional travelling expenses may be covered. Children undergoing work experience will not usually be covered by employer's liability or industrial injury protections (because the child is not 'in employment'), but the education authority is expected to take out adequate insurance for accidents or injuries during the work experience period.

Legal references used in this section

Section 1 of the Employment of Women, Young Persons and Children Act 1920

Sections 28-38 of the Children and Young Persons (Scotland) Act 1937, as amended.

Section 51 of the Merchant Shipping Act 1970

Employment of Children Act 1973

Section 123 of the Education (Scotland) Act 1980

Merchant Shipping (Employment of Young Persons) Regulations 1995

Children (Protection at Work) Regulations 1998

ENGLISH AS AN ADDITIONAL LANGUAGE

Parents have no general right to insist on their children being taught in the language of their choice (or even in the child's first language). The European Court of Human Rights have decided that the state can insist on teaching being provided in the majority language for the area. Parents' rights to have a child educated in accordance with their own religious or philosophical convictions do not apply to linguistic preferences.

Where other languages are widely used in an education authority's area, it should provide information for parents in those languages if necessary.

Children of "migrant" workers from EU countries have limited rights to some teaching in the host country in their native language. The host country must take appropriate measures to promote, alongside the regular curriculum, the teaching of the mother tongue and culture of the country of origin for such children.

Official guidance recommends that all pupils should have opportunities to reflect upon their own use of language and to develop "a conviction of the worth of their own accents and dialects". It also recommends that teachers should foster "respect for and interest in each pupil's mother tongue and its literature, whether English, Scots, Gaelic, Urdu, Punjabi, Cantonese or any other".

Children who are considered in law to be "in need" have additional rights. Services provided by the local authority (including education) must have due regard to the child's linguistic background, as far as is practicable.

If a child has difficulty in reaching their educational potential because English is not their first language, they may well have additional support needs (see **Additional Support for Learning**). This entitles the child to additional support, which may include input from an English as an Additional Language (or EAL) teacher.

For EAL/ Bilingual pupils who are at the early stages of learning English and are entered for SQA qualifications special exam arrangements may be made, such as the use of a bilingual dictionary. Parents should check with the Scottish Qualifications Authority and their school for more detailed information.

Education authorities should take steps to ensure that bilingual pupils are not treated less favourably or unfairly disadvantaged due to their linguistic abilities. A failure to do so could amount to unlawful race discrimination.

See also

Additional Support for Learning
Race discrimination
Standards in school education

Useful organisations

Enquire
Equalities and Human Rights Commission
Independent Special Education Advice (Scotland)
Parentzone
Scottish Qualifications Authority

Useful publications

Learning and Teaching Scotland *Learning in 2+ Languages* (available from Learning and Teaching Scotland

Legal references used in this section

Belgian Linguistic Case (No. 2) (1979-80) 1 EHRR 252

Council Directive 77/486/EEC of 25 July 1977 (on the education of the children of migrant workers)

Sections 22, 23, 93; Children (Scotland) Act 1995

The Education (National Priorities) (Scotland) Order 2000

Sections 1, 4 of the Education (Additional Support for Learning) (Scotland) Act 2004

EQUAL OPPORTUNITIES AND EQUALITY DUTIES

Each year the education authority must publish its education improvement objectives, which must include a statement of how it will improve equal opportunities and meet equal opportunities requirements.

There are now five main areas of discrimination that are unlawful, which apply to children in schools. These are discrimination on the grounds of:

- race (race, colour, nationality, citizenship, ethnic or national origin);
- sex (gender, marital status or transgender status);
- disability.
- religion or belief (including a lack of religion or belief); and
- sexual orientation.

Each of these is discussed within its own section in this book.

Human Rights

The Human Rights Act 1998 prohibits any discrimination which interferes with a pupil's right to access to education or other human rights on any of the following grounds: sex; race; colour; language; religion; political or other opinion; national origin; social origin; association with a national minority; property; birth; or any other status (which includes disability).

Equality duties

Public authorities, including education authorities, must comply with their equality duties, which impose certain legal responsibilities to actively promote equality of opportunity and eliminate discrimination. There are currently three equality duties:

- the race equality duty;
- the disability equality duty; and

• the gender equality duty.

The specific duties placed on schools are different from those on other public authorities.

The duties apply to education authorities and grant-aided schools, but not to independent schools.

Race equality duty

Education authorities and grant-aided schools have a statutory duty to promote race equality: this duty is known as the race equality duty.

The race equality duty helps to ensure that public authorities become accountable to the people they serve, to further equality of opportunity and improve race relations.

The general duty requires all public authorities to have due regard to the need to:

• eliminate unlawful racial discrimination;

• promote equality of opportunity; and

• promote good relations between persons of different racial groups.

Education authorities and grant-aided schools are also required to comply with certain specific duties:

• prepare a written race equality policy;

• keep a copy of the policy and, in the case of an education authority, ensure that each of its schools also keeps a copy;

• in the case of an education authority, ensure that each of its schools complies with the policy;

• assess the impact of its policies (including the race equality policy) on pupils, staff and parents of different racial groups including, in particular, the impact on attainment levels of such pupils; and

• monitor the impact of the operation of its policies on such pupils, staff and parents including, in particular, their impact on the attainment levels of such pupils.

Disability Equality Duty

The Disability Equality Duty requires all public bodies (including education authorities and grant-aided schools) to actively look at ways of ensuring that disabled people are treated equally. These bodies must also have produced and must implement a Disability Equality Scheme.

The general duty, requires public authorities in carrying out their functions to have due regard to the need to:

* promote equality of opportunity between disabled people and other people;

* eliminate discrimination that is unlawful under the Act;

* eliminate harassment of disabled people that is related to their disabilities;

* promote positive attitudes towards disabled people;

* encourage participation by disabled people in public life; and

* take steps to take account of disabled people's disabilities even where that involves treating disabled people more favourably than other people.

Education authorities and grant-aided schools are also covered by specific duties, which set out a framework to assist them in meeting their general duty. The specific duties are as follows:

* publish a Disability Equality Scheme which demonstrates how the authority or school intends to fulfil their general and specific duties;

* involve disabled people in the development of their Disability Equality Scheme. The Disability Equality Scheme must include a statement of:

  * the way in which disabled people have been involved in its development

  * the methods used for assessing both the impact and the likely impact of existing and new policies and practices, on equality for disabled people;

  * the steps which will be taken to fulfil the general duty (these steps must be detailed in an 'Action Plan' which is published as part of the Scheme);

- the arrangements you have made for gathering information on the effect of policies and practices on the educational opportunities available to, and on the achievements of, disabled pupils;
- the arrangements for putting the information gathered to use, in particular in reviewing the effectiveness of the Action Plans and subsequent Schemes.
- within three years of the Scheme being published, take the steps set out in the Action Plan (unless it is unreasonable or impracticable to do so) and put into effect the arrangements for gathering and making use of information;
- publish an annual report containing a summary of the steps taken under their Action Plans, the results of your information gathering and how you have used the information;
- make arrangements for all schools under the management of an education authority to:
  - assess the impact of their policies and practices, or the likely impact of proposed policies and practices, on equality for disabled pupils;
  - gather information on the effects of their policies and practices, the educational opportunities available and the achievements of disabled pupils
  - provide the authority with an annual report in respect of those two above matters;
  - carry out the steps which you propose to take towards the fulfilment of your general duty that need to be taken at school level; and
  - maintain a copy of the Scheme.

Public authorities should report annually on progress and be aware that organisations such as inspection bodies will be looking for evidence of progress, as will disabled people.

Gender equality duty

The gender equality duty requires education authorities and grant-aided schools to promote equality between men and women and eliminate unlawful sex discrimination. The duty places a legal responsibility on public authorities to demonstrate that they are actively promoting equality between men and women.

All public authorities must meet the general duty, which requires them to have due regard to the need to:

- eliminate unlawful sex discrimination and harassment; and
- promote equality of opportunity between men and women.

Public authorities in Scotland must also comply with their specific duty to:

- gather information on how their functions affect women and men;
- consult employees, service users, trade unions and other stakeholders;
- assess the different impact of policies and practices on both sexes;
- identify priorities and set gender equality objectives;
- plan and take action to achieve gender equality objectives;
- publish a gender equality scheme, report annually, and review progress every three years; and
- publish an equal pay policy statement (for listed authorities with more than 150 staff) by 28 September 2007, and report on progress every three years.

Education authorities are required, as well as publishing their own scheme, to ensure that the schools they manage gather information on the effects of their policies and practices on gender equality, assess the impact of those policies and practices on gender equality, carry out steps to meet the duty, and report on these activities.

There is also an additional duty on the Scottish ministers. From 1 July 2010, Scottish ministers will have to publish reports every three years that:

- set out the priority areas that ministers have identified for the advancement of gender equality by public authorities in Scotland; and

• provide a summary of progress made by public authorities in these priority areas.

• This duty is additional to the responsibility of the Scottish Executive under the specific duty to produce a gender equality scheme.

A failure to comply with one of the equality duties may lead to a legal challenge by way of judicial review, or enforcement action by the Equality and Human Rights Commission.

See also

Additional Support for Learning
Complaints
Consulting parents
Disability discrimination
Exclusion from school
Human rights
Legal action
Race discrimination
Religion or belief discrimination
Sex discrimination
Sexual orientation discrimination

Useful organisations

Enquire
Equalities and Human Rights Commission
Independent Special Education Advice (Scotland)
Parentzone

Useful publications

Equality and Human Rights Commission (2002) *The duty to promote race equality a guide for education authorities and schools in Scotland*

Equality and Human Rights Commission *(undated) Schools, education and the Disability Equality Duty: A guide to the Disability*

Equality Duty for education authorities and grant-aided schools in Scotland

Scottish Government (2007) *The Equality Act 2006: Guidance for Schools*

Legal references used in this section

Section 5; Standards in Scotland's Schools etc. (Scotland) Act 2000

EXAMINATIONS AND ASSESSMENT

From the moment children start at school, they will be going through a process of assessment (albeit a fairly informal one). A child's class teacher will make a regular note of his or her progress, and will tailor any individual learning programme to his or her needs and abilities. Each year, a formal record of a child's progress will be added to his or her school record. Parents will also be given the opportunity to keep up to date with their children's progress through parents' evenings and report cards. Outwith these times, a child's head teacher or class teacher will usually be happy to discuss the child's progress with their parent(s), although it is advisable to make an appointment in advance.

If the assessment process picks up on any concerns which may require additional support, the school will usually want to discuss these with a child's parents. Occasionally, children may be formally assessed with a view to establishing whether they have additional support needs and/or whether they require a Co-ordinated Support Plan. If this is the case, parents should be kept fully informed and involved (see **Additional Support for Learning** and **Co-ordinated Support Plans**).

Near the end of a child's second year at secondary school, parents will be asked to choose which subjects the child will take in the third and fourth years, with a view to sitting standard grades or acquiring other national qualifications. Some schools will offer a very wide range of subjects at this stage, while others (e.g. some smaller schools) may have a more limited range. If a child has a particular career in mind, the child can find out from the careers service which subjects would be beneficial. The choice of subjects is a clear example of the type of decision about which parents ought to consult their child. The school is not obliged to allow a child to take the subjects requested, but will usually accede to the parent's choice. If parents feel strongly that their child should be allowed to take a particular subject, they may discuss this initially with the relevant class teacher, then with the head teacher. If still dissatisfied, they may wish to take the matter up with the education authority.

Who is responsible for examinations?

Up until a child sits Standard Grades or other national exams, it is the education authority and the individual school who determine the timing and content of tests and exams. They will also determine the timing and content of any 'prelim' exams a child sits.

It is the responsibility of the Scottish Qualifications Authority to devise and develop qualifications, to mark candidates' exam papers and to award qualifications. The SQA is responsible for the content and time-tabling of the actual Standard Grades and National Qualifications examinations. Similar considerations apply to other qualification bodies.

What examinations do children sit?

At the end of fourth year, or sometimes earlier, a child will normally sit Standard Grades. Standard Grades can be sat at three different levels:

• Foundation (Grades 5-6);
• General (Grades 3-4); and
• Credit (grades 1-2).

Most pupils sit the general paper, and either the foundation or credit, according to their level of ability.

Once a child moves on a wide range of National Qualifications opens up, according to the child's ability. National Qualifications are offered at the following levels:

• Access;
• Intermediate 1;
• Intermediate 2;
• Higher; and
• Advanced Higher.

Which level a pupil sits in a particular subject will depend to some extent on the level of award he or she obtained at Standard Grade (if any). However, the subject teachers will be able to provide more detailed advice.

Able pupils can sit Standard Grades at the end of S3 and Highers at the end of S4.

If a child is absent from an exam, for example due to illness (a medical certificate will usually be required), it is possible for them to be awarded a qualification on the basis of classwork and other supporting documentation.

Special arrangements (e.g. scribing) can be made for pupils who have a disability which could hinder them in an exam.

If a child does not achieve the grades he or she was expected by the school to achieve, it is possible to appeal. This can only be done by the school and not by the individual concerned. The school will provide supporting information such as prelim papers and classwork. If parents believe this may be appropriate in their child's case, they should contact the school as soon as possible to discuss this. If an appeal is successful, a new certificate will be issued.

ASDAN Awards

Some schools in Scotland offer pupils an opportunity to achieve ASDAN awards and qualifications. ASDAN programmes seeks to recognise and reward skills and are often activity based. There are a wide range of awards for pupils of all abilities, including those with learning disabilities and other additional support needs.

ASDAN's Certificate of Personal Effectiveness (CoPE) has been accepted into the Scottish Credit and Qualifications Framework at levels 4,5 & 6. This is equivalent to Intermediate 1, 2 and Higher.

Scottish Baccalaureates

The Scottish Government has announced that a new Scottish Language Baccalaureate and a Scottish Science Baccalaureate will be introduced for pupils in S5 and S6 at schools in Scotland. These will include existing qualifications in science and languages at Higher and Advanced Higher level, together with an interdisciplinary project to be completed in S6. The first Baccalaureates are expected to be awarded in August 2010.

See also

Additional Support for Learning
Pupils' educational records

Useful organisations

ASDAN
Learning and Teaching Scotland
Scottish Qualifications Authority

Legal references used in this section

Part 1; Education (Scotland) Act 1996

Scottish Qualifications Authority Act 2002

EXCLUSION FROM SCHOOL

Decisions on exclusions are to be made on a case by case basis and no targets currently exist for reducing exclusions. During 2007/08 there were 44,794 exclusions from local authority schools in Scotland, most being temporary exclusions of male secondary school pupils.

Types of exclusion

The law does not make any distinction between types of exclusion, children are either excluded from school or not. However, education authorities refer to 'temporary exclusions' and 'exclusions/removal from the register':

• Temporary exclusions – where a child is excluded from the school but remains on the school's register as a pupil at that school and is expected to return;

• Removal from the Register - when a pupil is excluded from a school and the pupil's name is removed from the school register, the education authority having decided that the pupil should not return to that school.

There are also a number of other terms used to describe exclusion, including 'suspension', 'informal exclusion', 'cooling off period', 'sending a pupil home', 'permanent exclusion' and 'expulsion'. In Guidance to Education Authorities, the Scottish Government has stated that education authorities and schools should no longer use this terminology and that **all the above are forms of exclusion and must be recorded as such**.

Can the school just send a child home?

Schools should not just informally suspend or expel pupils. Any attempt to remove or ban a child from school is an exclusion and must be carried out according to statutory procedures. This applies even where the removal is only for a brief period (e.g. sending him or her home early from school for misbehaving), or where the education authority has made provision for a child to be educated at another school.

The education authority almost always allows the head teacher and senior management team of each school to make decisions about temporary exclusions. The power to exclude on a permanent basis is usually reserved to the Director of Education or other senior officials.

What about exclusion and human rights?

It is not, in principle, a breach of a child's human right to education to be excluded from a particular school. However, if the exclusion has the effect of preventing a child from attending another school, or if alternative education is not provided during a lengthy period of exclusion, then there may be a breach of human rights.

Grounds for exclusion

The education authority may exclude a child from school only where it thinks one of the following applies:

- the parent(s) have not complied with the school's rules (including disciplinary rules) or have prevented their child from complying with school rules or have allowed them to break school rules; or
- the child's continued attendance at school is likely to have a seriously detrimental effect on the school's order and discipline or on the education of its pupils.

Exclusion is a serious sanction and should be regarded as a last resort, for serious indiscipline, by schools and education authorities.

What about the child's education?

When a child is excluded from school, they still have a right to education and parents must ensure that they participate in any alternative education provision made available, in the same way they have a duty to ensure that their child attends school. If a child has been excluded from school, even temporarily, the education authority must (without undue delay) arrange for him or her to receive education – either at another school or elsewhere (e.g. at home). The provision of alternative education is an immediate requirement in the case of every pupil excluded from school. This is so that any detrimental effect on the excluded child is minimised. The Scottish Government circular on exclusions notes that while it is recognised that in certain cases, some delay may be unavoidable to enable appropriate arrangements to be put in place, it is expected that in all cases, those arrangements will be effective within 10 school days of the exclusion.

The Antisocial Behaviour etc (Scotland) Act 2004 makes provision for the Children's Reporter or a children's panel to refer a case to the Scottish Ministers where an education authority appears to be failing to provide education for an excluded pupil.

If a pupil is excluded from school and alternative education is to be provided outwith school, the authority should seek to provide the same quality, quantity and range of education as the pupil received prior to exclusion (if it is possible to do so).

Procedures for exclusion

Where a decision to exclude has been taken, the school (or the education authority) must:

On the same day, verbally or in writing:

- tell the parent(s) that their child has been excluded; and
- arrange a meeting within seven days to discuss the exclusion with them.

Within eight days, in writing, supply:

- the reasons why the child was excluded;
- the conditions for readmission of the child to school (if any);

- details of the parental right to appeal; and
- any other relevant information.

If a child returns to school within seven days or the child's parent indicates within that time that they don't wish to appeal, the "eight days" letter is not strictly required.

A failure to comply with these procedures will not usually, in itself, lead to an exclusion being overturned.

Conditions are commonly imposed for return to school. Usually, the parent and/or child will have to sign a document guaranteeing his or her future good behaviour. The courts have found this to be a lawful, even laudable, condition.

If a pupil is over school leaving age the information above must be given to him or her, instead of to the parent. If the school sends information about this type of exclusion to the parent, the pupil may have a valid complaint under the Data Protection Act.

Children who have legal capacity (see **Appeals**) also have the right to appeal against their own exclusion, but the information on the right to appeal and how to do so would still be sent to the parent(s). It is good practice for copies of all the above information to be sent to the child also, but not all authorities do this.

Guidance

In 2003, the then Scottish Executive published revised guidance about exclusion, which is designed to promote consistency in exclusion decisions across Scotland. Each education authority has their own guidance on exclusions which will be based on the national guidance. Parents should be able to obtain a copy of this local guidance directly from the education authority.

Education authorities will follow national guidance but may make additional guidelines for schools setting out local expectations on when exclusion is appropriate. The local guidelines may also describe the authority's expectations of how schools might take action on levels of indiscipline, before exclusion becomes the final resort.

For the appeal procedures see the section on **Appeals**. Parents or young persons have the right to appeal against an exclusion. In addition, children who have legal capacity have the right to appeal. A parent can appeal on behalf of a pupil who is older than school leaving age if the pupils is unable to do so due to a learning difficulty or mental incapacity.

The national guidance on exclusions states that either the child or the child's parent can appeal against an exclusion, but not both.

Who hears appeals?

An appeal will be heard, in the first instance, by the education appeal committee. After that, the parent, young person or child has a further right of appeal to the sheriff court, whose decision is final (subject to possible challenge by way of judicial review – see **Legal Action** for explanation of judicial review).

What can they decide?

Both the appeal committee and the sheriff court have the same powers:

• to uphold the exclusion;

• to quash the exclusion; or

• to uphold the exclusion, but alter the conditions for readmission to school.

Neither can alter the length of an exclusion. An appeal to the sheriff court, while kept relatively informal, is a complex legal procedure, and legal advice and representation should be sought from a solicitor familiar with education law. Legal Aid may be available.

What will they take into account?

In deciding whether or not an appeal against an exclusion should succeed, the sheriff will hear evidence from both sides and decide whether or not the decision to exclude was justified. The education appeal committee should take a similar approach.

School Records

Education authorities include details of any exclusions on a pupil's educational records. Details of previous exclusions may be used in making decisions about and appeals against new ones.

If the exclusion is overturned on appeal, then the record of the exclusion will be amended to show that it was overturned on appeal, and may not then be disclosed to any third party (e.g. in a job reference).

Special Circumstances

Where a child is "looked after" by the local authority, the education and social work departments ought to collaborate to make sure that the educational requirements of the child's Care Plan continue to be met even while excluded (see **Looked after children**).

Where an exclusion from school amounts to unlawful discrimination (on the grounds of sex, race, disability, religion or belief, or sexual orientation), then it may be possible to challenge the exclusion under that separate legislation instead of (or as well as) appealing.

The circumstances under which a pupil with additional support needs may be excluded are the same for any other pupil. However, alternative provision put in place must meet the pupil's educational and support needs. The availability of this must be considered where exclusion is thought to be necessary, but will not necessarily prevent an exclusion taking place. Schools and authorities are reminded by the national guidance that families may need support to cope with any stress caused by different patterns of attendance caused by an exclusion. The authority continues to have a duty to provide any support services normally provided to a child with additional support needs (e.g. speech and language therapy) while they are excluded.

See also

Additional Support for Learning
Appeals
Disability discrimination

Race discrimination
Religion or belief discrimination
Sex discrimination
Sexual orientation discrimination

Useful organisations

Enquire
Independent Special Education Advice (Scotland)
Parentzone

Legal references used in this section

Proudfoot v. Glasgow City Council 2003 SLT (Sh Ct) 23

X. v. United Kingdom; Appl. 13477/1987 Commission 4 October 1989

Abdul Hakim Ali v. The Headteacher and Governors of Lord Grey School [2004] EWCA Civ 382

Yanasik v. Turkey (1993) 74 DR 14

Campbell and Cosans v. United Kingdom (1982) 4 EHRR 293

Reg 4 of the Schools General (Scotland) Regulations 1975

Wyatt v. Wilson 1994 SLT 1135

D. v. Kennedy 1988 SLT 55

Section 14(3) of the Education (Scotland) Act 1980, inserted by Section 40 of the Standards in Scotland's Schools etc. (Scotland) Act 2000

Anti-Social Behaviour etc (Scotland) Act 2004

Reg 4A of the Schools General (Scotland) Regulations 1975

Glasgow City Council, Petitioners, Court of Session 15 Jan 2004

Wyatt v. Wilson 1994 SLT 1135

Exclusion from Schools in Scotland: Guidance to Education Authorities – SEED Circular 8/03

Section 28H(1)-(4) of the Education (Scotland) Act 1980

Section 41 of the Standards in Scotland's Schools etc. (Scotland) Act 2000

Section 28H(6)-(7) of the Education (Scotland) Act 1980

Section 28F(3),(4),(8)&(9) of the Education (Scotland) Act 1980

Wallace v. Dundee City Council 2000 SLT (Sh Ct) 60

FEES AND CHARGES

School education provided by the education authority must be offered free of charge. Parents cannot be charged for tuition for courses taught in the school or for things like books, materials and equipment or other articles which a pupil needs to take full advantage of their school education.

Nursery education provided by the education authority must be free of charge for children of the ages set down by law (approx. 3-5 years old, but see section on **School Starting Age**).

However, examples of when fees and charges can be made include:

- the use of social, cultural or recreational facilities, such as community education premises, or sports or leisure equipment or centres;
- specialist lessons for music or other subjects if these are provided at a more advanced level than at other schools;
- an education authority providing school education (including any additional support) for a pupil who lives outwith their area – any fees it charges will usually be met by the pupil's own education authority;
- education authority nursery or pre-school education which is over and above that which it has to provide by law;
- where a fee is charged for classes, then the education authority may also make a charge for books, materials or equipment needed for those classes;
- extra-curricular activities like school trips or additional tuition out of school times (however, these must always be optional, and suitable alternative arrangements must be available for those who do not take part in such activities); and

• the authority ordinarily has to charge for school meals, where these are provided to pupils who are not entitled to free meals (see **Food and Drink**).

The education authority can award scholarships to any pupil in their fee-charging classes, to cover all or part of the fee. A scholarship may only be awarded on the grounds of the pupil's aptitude and ability.

Independent Schools

Independent schools are allowed to charge fees for education, limited only by what parents are prepared to pay.

See also

Admission to school
Books, materials and equipment
Food and Drink
Independent schools
Pre-school education

Useful organisations:

Citizens Advice Scotland
Scottish Council of Independent Schools

Legal references used in this section

Sections 1, 3, 11, 23, 24, 75A; Education (Scotland) Act 1980, as amended

Section 33 of the Standards in Scotland's Schools etc. (Scotland) Act 2000

FINANCE AND FUNDING OF EDUCATION

Education authority schools

Education authority schools receive the vast majority of their funding from the local authority itself. The local authority receives its funding from the Scottish Government and from local taxation such as council tax. Each year, the council will make projections on how much it will need to spend during the next financial year in all of its departments. It then sets its council tax rates at a level which will make up the deficit between the amount of funding it will receive from central government and the amount it has projected it will need to provide services throughout the next year. Local authorities have a general duty to ensure that their resources are used economically, efficiently and effectively. Each year, local authorities must publish annual abstracts of accounts. Parents are entitled to a copy of these. If a local resident objects to anything in the accounts, on the basis that the money has been spent negligently or unlawfully, the resident can make written objections to the auditor within 14 days of the publication of the accounts.

It is very much in the discretion of the local authority how much of its revenue is spent on education, provided that it meets all of its statutory duties. The education committee will set the education budget for each financial year. This will take into account the money needed for salaries, books and equipment, and maintenance costs. Parents can get access to the reports and minutes of education committees and sub-committees, to find out what the expenditure projections and breakdowns are for the education budget. As a result of the "concordat" between the Scottish Government and local authorities, much less of the central grant received by local authorities is "ring-fenced" meaning that authorities have more discretion in allocating the resources they receive. Each Council is to enter into a Single Outcome Agreement with the Scottish Government setting out national and local outcomes to be achieved, including education outcomes.

Some education authorities have initiated "Public Private Partnerships" or "Private Finance Initiative" in a bid to improve schools. Under these schemes, companies either build new schools or carry out extensive improvements to existing schools and invest in modern technology. The education authority then leases the schools and equipment from the companies over a period of several years. During this period, the companies maintain the buildings and equipment, and are responsible for cleaning and other services. At the end of the lease period, the buildings will transfer to education authority ownership. Although the buildings are not owned and maintained by the education authority during the period of the lease, the authority has the same responsibilities towards the pupils attending these schools as it would if they did own the buildings.

The Scottish Government has announced their intention to depart from the above methods of utilising private finance in favour of a Scottish Futures Trust, which will make use of non-profit distributing principles (NDP).

Independent schools

Independent schools receive no funding from local or central government. They generate their income from the fees charged for pupils' attendance. Occasionally, a child may be placed in an independent school by an education authority. In this situation, the education authority will pay the school fees to the independent school directly.

Other sources of funding for schools

Both local authority and independent schools may receive other income or property from, for example, educational endowments (usually made by charities or foundations), bequests from private individuals, donations from individuals or businesses and from money raised by pupils and parents. Recently, some private companies have begun to sponsor certain facilities within schools (such as school canteens). Parents may be consulted if the school is considering taking on such a sponsorship; however there is no requirement for consultation. If parents object to a proposed sponsorship arrangement, they could take this up with the head teacher or the education authority. In such a situation, it would be worthwhile finding out whether other parents also object. Such matters could be raised through the Parent Council if the school has one. The Scottish Consumer Council (now Consumer Focus Scotland) has produced guidance on sponsorship in schools which may be of interest.

See also

Education authorities
Independent schools

Useful organisations

Scottish Council of Independent Schools
Scottish Parent Teacher Council
Parentzone

Useful publications

Scottish Parent Teacher Council (undated) *A Simple Guide to Money Matters*

Consumer Focus Scotland (2008) *Guidelines on Commercial Sponsorship in the Public Sector*

Scottish Consumer Council (2004) *Guidelines on Commercial Activities in Schools* (available from Consumer Focus Scotland)

FINANCIAL ASSISTANCE

Education Maintenance Allowance (EMA)

Higher school bursaries have now been phased out and replaced by an Education Maintenance Allowance (EMA). EMA is available across Scotland to eligible pupils in fifth and sixth year at school and some students in further education.

The Education Maintenance Allowance is a weekly payment of up to £30, paid directly to young people who stay on in full-time education after school leaving age. There are also biannual bonuses of £150 which are conditional on good educational progress.

EMA entitlement is based on household income and young people from households with annual incomes up to approximately £32,000 should be eligible.

Local authorities administer the EMA for those in school and the Scottish Further Education Funding Council (SFEFC) for those at college. Application forms and more information are available directly from schools and colleges. The local authority or college will notify all applicants about whether or not they are entitled to an EMA. Payments start once the young person has enrolled at school or college and has started studies for that year. Payments are made fortnightly directly to the young person's bank account.

Other Assistance

Provisions relating to school clothing grants, assistance with travelling expenses and free school meals apply equally to pupils over school leaving age as to those under school leaving age, and are not affected by receipt of an education maintenance allowance.

See also

Clothing and uniform
Food and drink
Transport

Useful organisations

Citizens Advice Scotland
Education Maintenance Allowance Scotland

FLEXI-SCHOOLING

What is Flexi-schooling?

Flexi-schooling is where parents and a local school share the job of teaching a child in an agreed partnership set out in a contract drawn up between the two. Parents, who would otherwise be quite content to home educate, may wish their child to be able to take advantage of certain educational resources only practically available through the school.

Flexi-schooling is practised by some local authorities in England & Wales, where the concept of authorised absences is provided for by law. There, as in Scotland, flexi-schooling is only possible with the active support and permission of the education authority.

Do parents have a right to Flexi-school?

No. Legally, if children attend an education authority school, their parents' obligation is to ensure that the children attend regularly. Any absence without reasonable excuse leaves the parents open to prosecution. There is no legal provision for a "third way".

However, parents' right to educate their children in accordance with their own wishes might be accommodated by a school if it treats certain pupil absences as if that pupil were present at school, and agrees to record them as authorised absences. This may apply where the absence has been authorised and parents comply with any conditions set by the education authority.

Additional Support Needs

Where a child or young person who is home educated has additional support needs, the education authority has a discretionary power to provide appropriate additional support to the child or young person. This discretion must be exercised reasonably.

See also

Additional Support for Learning
Attendance and absence
Home education

Useful organisations

Enquire
Independent Special Education Advice (Scotland)
Parentzone
Schoolhouse Home Education Association

Legal references used in this section

Section 28(1) of the Education (Scotland) Act 1980

Reg 9; Sched 1 of the Schools General (Scotland) Regulations 1984

Section 5(4) of the Education (Additional Support for Learning) (Scotland) Act 2004

FOOD AND DRINK

The education authority has powers to provide food and drink to pupils at their schools. The authority must charge for school lunches (except for free school lunches – see below). Food or drink provided to pupils at other times can be free of charge or may be charged for. Where food or drink is charged for, the authority must charge pupils the same price for the same quantities of food and drink. Therefore, the authority can provide free breakfast to pupils, but not universal free lunches.

The education authority must also provide facilities for pupils to eat food and drink brought by them into school (e.g. a dining hall for packed lunches). Education authorities also have the power to provide food and drink at other schools, though this is rarely, if ever, done.

Education authorities must promote the availability of school lunches in public schools and encourage pupils to eat school lunches.

Free School Lunches

Education authorities must provide, free of charge, sufficient food and drink in the middle of the day for pupils at their schools who are, or whose parents are, in receipt of Income Support, Income-based Jobseekers' Allowance, or given support under the Immigration and Asylum Act 1999.

Free school lunches are also available where a pupil or a pupil's parents are in receipt of a Child Tax Credit (but not in receipt of a Working Tax Credit) and the award is based on an annual income which is less than the income threshold for Child Tax Credits.

The Scottish Ministers also have powers to make regulations specifying other benefits, allowances or tax credits which would confer eligibility to free school lunches.

Education authorities must take reasonable steps to ensure that every pupil who is entitled to receive free school lunches, receives them.

In October 2007, the Scottish Government passed regulations to allow the trial of free school lunches for all pupils in P1-P3 in five local authorities (East Ayrshire, Fife, Glasgow, Scottish Borders and West Dunbartonshire). The trial came to an end on 30th June 2008. At the time of writing the full findings from the monitoring of the trial had not been published.

Health and Nutrition

The Scottish Ministers, education authorities and the managers of grant-aided schools must, by law, endeavour to ensure that the schools they are responsible for are health-promoting schools. This duty also applies to hostels provided for pupil accommodation by an education authority. A school or hostel is health-promoting if it provides activities, an environment and facilities which promote the physical, social, mental and emotional health and wellbeing of pupils.

Education authority schools and hostels and grant-aided schools must ensure that food and drink provided complies with nutritional regulations.

These current regulations came into force on 4 August 2008 for Primary Schools and are due to come into force on 3 August 2009 for Secondary School. They prescribe various detailed nutritional requirements for food and drink in schools. Parents should consult the guidance document (see below) for the full details.

Requirements for school lunches include:

• Not less than 2 types of vegetable (not including potatoes) shall be provided every day.

- Not less than 2 types of fruit shall be provided every day.
- Bread shall be provided every day.
- Oily fish must be provided at least once every 3 weeks.
- No savoury snacks shall be provided except:savoury crackers; oatcakes; or breadsticks.
- No confectionery shall be provided and cakes, biscuits and puddings must not contain any confectionery.
- Deep fried food shall not be provided more than 3 times in a week.
- Chips may only be served as an accompaniment to other food.

Further nutritional standards are imposed, including a list of permitted drinks, which effectively bans fizzy drinks from school canteens.

The regulations do not apply to food or drink provided to any food or drink provided–

- by parents or pupils (e.g. packed lunches);
- at any social, cultural or recreational event;
- to mark any religious or cultural occasion;
- for use in teaching food preparation and cookery skills (e.g. in home economics classes); or
- as part of a medically recommended diet for any pupil.

Schools must ensure that drinking water is provided free of charge at all times to pupils on the premises of public schools.

Policy information

The education authority must provide written information on its general policy on school meals, and the arrangements made at each school, and this information must be made available to parents on request.

See also

Fees and Charges
Financial Assistance

Useful organisations

Citizens Advice Scotland
Parentzone
Scottish Government

Useful publications

Scottish Government (2008) *Healthy Eating in Schools: A Guide to Implementing the Nutritional Requirements for Food and Drink in Schools (Scotland) Regulations* 2008

Legal references used in this section

Sections 53, 55; 56 A–D of the Education (Scotland) Act 1980

Section 2A of the Standards in Scotland's Schools etc. Act 2000

Education (School Meals) (Scotland) Act 2003

Schools (Health Promotion and Nutrition) (Scotland) Act 2007

Education (School and Placing Information) (Scotland) Regulations 1982 [Schedule 1; paras 2(m) & 3(s)]

Education (School Meals) (Scotland) Regulations 2003

Provision of School Lunches (Disapplication of the Requirement to Charge) (Scotland) Order 2007

Nutritional Requirements for Food and Drink in Schools (Scotland) Regulations 2008

GAELIC

Gaelic

Education authorities must provide the teaching of Gaelic at schools in Gaelic-speaking areas. The phrase "Gaelic-speaking areas" is not defined, but would include the Highlands (except Caithness), the Western Isles and some parts of Argyll.

The education authority must give parents written information (in both Gaelic and English, where appropriate) about schools in its area which have Gaelic teaching. Their annual statement of education improvement objectives must include details of how or in what circumstances it will provide Gaelic-medium education. Where Gaelic-medium education is provided, the education authority must include details of how it will try to develop this.

The National Priorities in Education currently include paying particular attention to Gaelic. The performance measures for the National Priorities include the number and percentage of written requests for Gaelic medium education met by each authority.

The United Kingdom is party to the Council of Europe's Charter for Regional and Minority Languages and the Council's Committee of Experts has recommended that in order to more fully comply with the undertakings given under that Charter, the Scottish Government "make primary and secondary education in Scottish Gaelic generally available in the areas where the language is used".

Gaelic as a subject is available at Standard Grade, Access, Intermediate 1 and 2, Higher and Advanced Higher. Pupils at present may (when requested) sit Standard Grade exams in Gaelic for Geography, History, Maths and Modern Studies.

Gaelic medium education

The Scottish Executive issued guidance to education authorities in 2004 on Gaelic education. That guidance recognised that Gaelic medium education is both essential to the future of Gaelic in Scotland and a legitimate expectation of the Gaelic speaking community in Scotland.

The guidance asks authorities which receive specific grant funding for Gaelic education to prepare a policy statement on Gaelic medium education. The policy statement would now be included in a Gaelic language plan (see below) where one has been adopted by the authority.

Where an authority has a policy statement on Gaelic medium education, it should include the following:

Pre-school and Primary

- a commitment to promote and publicise Gaelic medium education;
- a commitment to develop Gaelic medium provision at pre-school, primary and secondary levels and to support Gaelic in the home;
- a commitment to deliver Gaelic medium education as an entitlement at pre-school and primary wherever reasonable demand exists;
- an explanation of how the authority has chosen to define reasonable demand, in terms of numbers of pupils, availability and travel to schools, school stages and any other factors;
- a description of at how English will be introduced to Gaelic medium classes at primary.

Secondary

- a commitment to make use of ICT in the delivery of secondary Gaelic courses;
- a commitment to provide a minimum of two secondary subjects in Gaelic for pupils that have gone through Gaelic medium primary education.

Support for Pupils

- a commitment to ensure good quality materials are available for the delivery of subjects through the medium of Gaelic;
- a commitment to establish a bi-lingual ethos in schools that have Gaelic medium classes;
- a commitment to provide Gaelic extra-curricular activities for Gaelic medium education pupils;
- a statement on transport to school for pupils in Gaelic medium education;
- a commitment to provide additional support in Gaelic for Gaelic medium pupils where required or appropriate.

Support for Teachers

- a commitment to ensure that Gaelic teachers receive Gaelic CPD;
- a commitment to ensure that Gaelic teacher supply provision is available;
- a commitment to support the training of teachers who would like to transfer to Gaelic medium education.

Bòrd na Gàidhlig

Bòrd na Gàidhlig was established by the Gaelic Language (Scotland) Act 2005 which aims to promote the use of Scottish Gaelic, secure the status of the language and ensure its long-term future.

The Act sets out 3 main aims for Bòrd na Gàidhlig:

- to increase the number of persons who are able to use and understand the Gaelic language;
- to encourage the use and understanding of the Gaelic language; and
- to facilitate access, in Scotland and elsewhere, to the Gaelic language and Gaelic culture.

Bòrd na Gàidhlig has prepared a detailed National Gaelic Education Strategy as part of the National Plan for Gaelic.

Bòrd na Gàidhlig has been charged with identifying public authorities to develop Gaelic Language Plans. Among the 32 education authorities in Scotland, at the time of writing, three had prepared Gaelic Language Plans, and had those plans approved by the Bòrd: The Highland Council, Argyll & Bute Council and Comhairle nan Eilean Siar.

Where a local authority has a Gaelic Language Plan, the provision of Gaelic as a subject and Gaelic medium education will form an important part of the authority's plan.

Useful organisations

Bòrd na Gàidhlig
Comann nam Pàrant
Lagh–Sgoile

Useful publications :

Scottish Executive (2004) *Education Guidance Issued Under Section 13 of the Standards in Scotland's Schools etc Act 2000 on Gaelic Education* (available from the Scottish Government)

Legal references used in this section

Section 1(5); Education (Scotland) Act 1980

Reg 13(3); Sched I(3)(n); Education (School and Placing Information) (Scotland) Regulations 1982

Sections 4(1), 5(2)(c); Standards in Scotland's Schools etc. Act 2000

The Education (National Priorities) (Scotland) Order 2000

Gaelic Language (Scotland) Act 2005

GRANT-AIDED SCHOOLS

In addition to schools which are managed by the education authorities, and independent schools, there are 8 grant-aided schools in Scotland. All but one of Scotland's grant-aided schools are special schools, catering for a range of additional support needs and disabilities. The grant-aided special schools are:

- Donaldson's College;
- The Royal Blind School;
- Harmeny Education Trust;
- East Park School;
- The Scottish Centre for Children with Motor Impairments (Craighalbert Centre);
- Corseford Residential School; and
- Stanmore House.

Roughly 50% of the total costs of educating children in these schools is met by grants from the Scottish Government; the remaining proportion is met by the education authority.

Placement in these schools is generally made at the discretion of the education authority. Pupils with additional support needs may also be placed in grant-aided special schools (if the school is willing to offer them a place) by way of a placing request. A placing request for a grant-aided special school may be refused by an education authority if:

- they can meet the pupil's needs in another school (whether or not that school is run by the authority);
- they have offered the pupil a place in that school; and
- it is not reasonable, considering the respective costs and

suitability, to place the pupil in the grant-aided school. (See **Additional Support for Learning**).

If a placing request is accepted by the education authority or is successful on appeal, the education authority must place the pupil in the grant-aided school and meet the fees and any other necessary costs of attendance of the pupil there.

Her Majesty's Inspectorate of Education (HMIE) inspects grant-aided schools in the same way that it inspects education authority schools and independent schools. See **Inspection** and **inspector's reports** for further information.

Jordanhill School

Jordanhill School was once run and operated by Jordanhill Teacher Training College as a demonstration school. When it was decided that this was no longer needed, the local authority was offered but did not wish to take over the running of the school.

Therefore, it is now financed directly by grants from the Scottish Government. It is the only grant-aided mainstream school in Scotland. Jordanhill School is a company limited by guarantee. No fees are paid for attendance at the school nor are there academic criteria for entry. By regulations, the Scottish Ministers are empowered to award one-off grants to cover such expenditure as:

• purchasing land and buildings;

• building, enlarging and improving buildings;

• supplying equipment and furnishings;

• providing for and laying out of premises, including playing fields etc.; and

• other work of a permanent nature.

The Scottish Ministers are also empowered to make recurring grants to cover things like:

• administration costs;

• maintenance of the school; and

• staff costs etc.

Payment of grants is subject to certain conditions being met. The Scottish Ministers have to be satisfied as to the company's financial stability, its fitness to receive grants, and its competence to manage the school.

Jordanhill School has to comply with certain areas of the law relating to school premises and the conduct of the school. It must also supply in writing to the parents of pupils (or prospective pupils) at the school, on request, specified information about the school.

See also

Additional Support for Learning

Useful organisations

Enquire
Independent Special Education Advice (Scotland)
HM Inspectorate of Education
Parentzone

Legal references used in this section

The Jordanhill School Grant Regulations 1988

GUIDANCE / PASTORAL CARE

Children may from time to time need guidance from school or other staff about:

• their studies and which courses or subjects to choose;

• any personal problems they may be having at school; or

• choosing a career or deciding what to do after leaving school.

The education authority must have written information for parents about the guidance provided at each of its secondary schools. Specialist staff are appointed at secondary schools to provide guidance. In primary schools the head teacher or other staff may also be able to offer guidance.

Guidance teachers

All education authority secondary schools in Scotland have guidance teachers. Their job is:

• to help pupils decide about what subjects to choose for standard grades, highers and other courses, and to monitor their progress and attainment (educational guidance);

• to help pupils with any personal problems, such as bullying or settling in (personal guidance); and

• to help pupils decide about careers and/or further or higher education (careers guidance).

Guidance teachers sometimes also teach programmes of personal and social education, which deal with health, relationships and careers.

Educational guidance

The education authority can offer guidance about the education made available to pupils. Most secondary schools will make arrangements to advise and consult pupils and parents about decisions relating to what subjects to study, what exams to take, and education after school leaving age.

Personal guidance

Children should be given personal guidance to help them cope with any problems they are having, including ones to do with settling in when starting school or moving school, study problems (e.g. poor concentration), or trouble with fellow pupils (e.g. bullying or victimisation). This aspect of guidance is also known as pastoral care.

Careers guidance

Careers advice and information must be made available to children before leaving school or further education to help them choose a suitable career. This should take into account the child's capabilities and the training needed for a particular career. Careers advice may continue to be given once a child has left school. A record must be kept of any vocational advice given to a child.

Children may be given the opportunity to go on a work experience course before leaving school.

Psychological Service

The education authority must provide its own psychological service, staffed by educational and child psychologists, trained to deal with any behavioural or learning difficulties. Psychologists have special responsibility for attending to any special educational needs (or additional support needs) a child might have, but they may also become involved if a child is having discipline problems in class. A child may be referred by the school for clinical observation and parents can request assessments which, if reasonable, should be complied with.

See also

Additional support needs
Careers education
Information for parents

Useful organisations

Careers Scotland
Childline
Enquire
Independent Special Education Advice (Scotland)
Parentline
Parentzone

Useful publications

Scottish Executive (2005) *Supporting pupils: A study of guidance and pupil support in Scottish schools* (available from the Scottish Government)

Legal references used in this section

Sections 8 to 10A; Employment and Training Act 1973, as amended

Sections 4, 61; Education (Scotland) Act 1980

HEALTH

Medical and dental examinations

The education authority has a number of rights and responsibilities in relation to children's health. Firstly, it can ask parents to present their children for medical or dental examination. It may do this, for example, if parents claim their children are too ill to attend school. If a parent fails to comply with such a requirement, they may face criminal prosecution.

Secondly, "in the interests of cleanliness", education authorities may authorise a medical officer to examine the bodies and/or clothing of all pupils, some pupils or an individual pupil at a school. Female pupils must be examined by a female medical officer. If the examination finds a pupil to be "infested with vermin", or "otherwise in a foul condition", then the education authority may issue a notice on the parent (or the pupil if over school leaving age) requiring treatment or cleansing to be carried out within 24 hours. If the problem is not put right within 24 hours, the education authority can then issue a notice requiring the pupil to be cleansed or treated, and this would give authority for the pupil to be treated.

It is worth noting, however, that if a child has a sufficient level of understanding to consent to medical treatment and procedures, then any medical examination or treatment can only be carried out if he or she consents. Children are generally considered to have sufficient levels of understanding at 12 years old.

Head lice alerts

Scottish Government guidance recommends that 'alert letters' are not sent to the parents of other children in the class of a child who may be infected with head lice. 'Alert letters' may lead parents to believe that there is an 'outbreak' when, in fact, only one child is infected. Parents might then treat their own child unnecessarily. The parents of a child who appears to have a head lice infection should, however, be informed.

Schools may issue general information on the detection and treatment of head lice.

Other infestations etc.

If the medical officer has reason to believe that a pupil is infested with vermin or otherwise in a foul condition, but arrangements cannot be made for him/her to be examined or treated straight away, then the education authority may exclude the pupil from school until the pupil can be examined or treated. This will **not** be valid in the case of a head lice infection. If a pupil is excluded from school in these circumstances, then the period of exclusion will be seen as absence with a reasonable excuse, unless the pupil's infestation is as a result of some "wilful default" on the part of the parent or young person.

If a pupil is repeatedly found to be infested, this may lead to the parent's prosecution (or the pupil's if over school leaving age). Repeated infestation may also be mentioned in grounds for referral to a children's hearing.

Immunisation

As part of the immunisation programme, arrangements are made for immunisation of children of school age to take place within schools. If a child is due to be immunised, parents will be notified and should be given information about the proposed immunisation and given a consent form to complete and return. Parents are under no obligation to have their children immunised, and a child will not be immunised without consent. However, if a child is old enough to give consent, the child may do so even where the parent objects.

Health in the curriculum

As part of their general duties towards pupils, education authorities often introduce health issues into the school curriculum. For example, the dangers associated with smoking and drug and alcohol abuse, as well as sexual health matters, may feature in some classes. The type of information a child receives will depend on what stage of schooling he or she is at.

School nurses are qualified registered nurses, employed by the Health Board to work with pupils, teachers and parents in promoting the health of children at school. This may include health education on issues such as smoking, drugs or sexual health. School nurses may provide support for children with medical needs like asthma, diabetes or epilepsy. This may include working with school staff to help them understand the health needs of individual children. They will also be involved in immunisation and vaccination programmes at school.

Additional support needs

Where a Health Board may be able to assist an education authority with their additional support needs functions (e.g. by arranging to assess a particular child or to make provision of therapies at a special school), the authority may make a formal statutory request for help from the Health Board. The Health Board must comply with such a request unless it is incompatible with its own statutory or other duties, or unduly prejudices the discharge of any of its functions. The deadline for comply with a request for help is 10 weeks, although this can be extended under certain specified circumstances to a maximum of 16 weeks.

See also

Additional Support for Learning
Attendance and absence
Children's hearings
Medical attention
Sex education

Useful organisations

Enquire
Independent Special Education Advice (Scotland)
Parentzone

Useful publications

Scottish Executive (2001) *Administration of medicines in schools* (available from the Scottish Government)

Legal references used in this section

Section 57, 58, 131A of the Education (Scotland) Act 1980

Section 2(4) of the Age of Legal Capacity (Scotland) Act 1991

HOLIDAYS

School Holidays

Schools must normally be open for at least 190 days (excluding Saturdays and Sundays) in any school year. In Scotland, the school year normally runs from mid-August to late June or early July the following year. There are traditionally school holidays in the summer, late autumn, Christmas and Easter, plus various shorter one-day or long weekend holidays.

School opening, closing and holiday dates are fixed by the education authority, and it must inform parents of these dates. Different holiday arrangements may exist for different areas or schools within the same authority. Local Authority websites normally provide this information.

The education authority may alter the dates of the school session at its discretion. However, where it wants to make a drastic change to a long-standing holiday, it may have to consult with parents before doing so.

Independent schools are responsible for deciding their own opening and closing dates and holidays. They do not have to stay open for 190 school days, although the Scottish Ministers will need to be satisfied as to the standard of education provided in order for the school to remain registered.

In exceptional circumstances the school may stay open for fewer than 190 days a year: for example, as a result of industrial action, fire damage, or some other reason beyond the education authority's control.

Family holidays

Parents have a legal duty to see that their children continue to attend school regularly, except where there is a reasonable excuse for their absence (such as illness). There may be occasions, however, when parents wish or need to take their children on holiday or away from school during term time.

Parents should write to the school asking permission to do this, and give the reasons for their request. Requests for absence for relevant religious holidays should normally be granted. Most family holidays taken during term time will be categorised as an unauthorised absence.

However, schools may, under exceptional circumstances, authorise a family holiday during term time. For example, a family holiday may be important to the well-being of a family following serious or terminal illness, bereavement or other traumatic events. Family holidays during term-time may also be authorised where evidence is provided by an employer that it cannot accommodate leave during school holidays without serious consequences.

If prior permission is not sought, the holiday will be automatically recorded as an unauthorised absence. In serious or repeated cases, action may be taken against parents for their child's non-attendance at school.

See also

Attendance and absence

Useful organisations

Parentzone

Useful publications

Scottish Executive (2007) *Included, Engaged and Involved: Guidance on the management of attendance and absence in Scottish schools* (available from the Scottish Government)

Legal references used in this section

Reg 5, 9, Sch. 1; Schools General (Scotland) Regulations 1975

Schedule 1, 2(o); Education (School and Placing Information) (Scotland) Regulations 1982

Section 35; Education (Scotland) Act 1980

HOME EDUCATION

Education is compulsory but school is not. While parents have to make sure their children receive education, this does not necessarily mean sending them to school. Some parents choose to educate their children at home instead.

What is home education?

Home education is the term used for parents educating their children at home rather than by sending them to school. It covers a wide variety of styles of educating, from formal school-type lessons to a more flexible, child-led approach to learning.

In Scots law, a child's education is their parent's responsibility. Not for nothing are teachers sometimes described as acting *in loco parentis*. Parents are under a duty to provide their children with education. Most parents fulfil this duty by sending their children to school. However, the law provides for two choices, each as valid as the other:

• by attendance of the child at a education authority school; or

• by other means (including independent schools and home education).

It is important to remember that the law says that, as a general rule, children should be educated according to their parents' wishes. The European Convention of Human Rights says that children are to be educated in a way which guarantees respect for their parents' religious or philosophical convictions. However, these rights are limited by the stipulation that the education provided must be both "suitable" and "efficient" and be consistent with the avoidance of unreasonable public expenditure.

Is permission needed to home educate?

No, parents do not require consent to educate their children at home. However, if a child has attended an education authority school, then permission is required to remove the child from that school. Permission should not be withheld unreasonably.

In normal circumstances, consent to withdraw a child from school in order to home educate them should be granted immediately. If there are concrete child protection issues or evidence to suggest that an efficient education may not be provided, then the education authority may first gather more relevant information (including the views of the child) before coming to a decision. Irregular attendance at school is not of itself a reason to withhold consent. The decision should be reached as quickly as possible and given in writing to the parent(s). The aim should be to issue a decision within 6 weeks of the receipt of the original application. The parent(s) should be given an opportunity to address the grounds for refusal and resubmit their request for reconsideration.

Is the education authority still involved?

Whether a child has been withdrawn from school or not, the education authority is likely to take an interest in any decision to home educate. Many parents resent this, seeing it as an unwelcome and unwarranted intrusion into their home.

However, Scottish Government guidance suggests that education authorities ought to request an update from home educating families on an annual basis. Only where there is cause for concern would more regular reports be required. The education authority has no right to demand access to the family home, nor to see the child, in order to assess their education. Refusal to allow such access is not, in itself, to be regarded as cause for concern regarding the efficiency and suitability of the home education provided.

Nonetheless, the education authority must be satisfied that the education being providing at home is both efficient and suitable to the child's age, aptitude and ability. If parents are able to demonstrate that this is the case at an early stage, this precludes the need to do so before a committee of the education authority or the sheriff court.

What sort of home education is required?

As mentioned above, the required standard for home education ("suitable" and "efficient") has not been clearly defined, either by Parliament or by the courts. In practice, there are a wide variety of educational styles employed by home educators. There may be an absence of any kind of formal assessment, but the education authority should assume that the education being provided is both efficient and suitable, unless there is evidence to the contrary.

Scottish Government guidance suggests that efficient and suitable education should include:

• consistent parental involvement;

• recognition of the child's needs, attitudes and aspirations;

• involvement in a broad spectrum of activities; and

• access to appropriate resources and materials.

It is not necessary for home education to be geared toward achieving any kind of recognised academic qualification, although some of these are accessible to home educated children.

What are the education authority's powers?

If the education authority is not satisfied that children are receiving suitable and efficient education, it will ask their parent(s) to appear before a committee to assess whether or not the education provided at home meets these required standards. An education authority should only begin down this route if it has first given the parent a written report on why it is not satisfied as to the education, and also afforded them an opportunity to respond to such concerns. If parent's prefer, they can request this information in writing rather than appearing at the committee.

If the education authority is not satisfied following the committee's consideration, then it must serve an attendance order on the parent. This order requires the parent to send the child to the school named within the order.

There is a right of appeal against the attendance order to the sheriff court. An appeal is only likely to be successful if the education authority has improperly exercised its decision-making powers. This is a somewhat complex area and legal advice on the subject should be sought.

The European Court of Human Rights has confirmed that it is not a breach of the parental rights to respect for their philosophical convictions to require parents to co-operate with an assessment of a home educated child's educational attainment.

Non-attendance at school

If a child is withdrawn from school without consent, or an attendance order has been served, then any failure to attend school is likely to be "without reasonable excuse". The fact that a child is receiving what may be an excellent education at home instead does not alter this.

If a child is not attending school regularly – without reasonable excuse – then the education authority can take criminal legal proceedings against the parent(s) or refer the child's case to the Reporter to the Children's Panel (see **Children's Hearings**).

See also

Appeals
Attendance and absence
Children's Hearings

Useful organisations

Parentzone
Schoolhouse Home Education Association

Useful publications

Scottish Consumer Council (2008) *Home-based Education: Towards Positive Partnerships* (available from Consumer Focus Scotland)

Scottish Executive (2007) *Home Education Guidance* (available from the Scottish Government)

Legal references used in this section

Sections 28, 30, 35, 37, 38, 42; Education (Scotland) Act 1980

Section 53; Children (Scotland) Act 1995

Section 14; Standards in Scotland's Schools etc. Act 2000

Article 2, Protocol 1; European Convention on Human Rights

Parlane v. Perth & Kinross Joint County Council 1954 SLT (Sh Ct) 95

Family H v. United Kingdom (1984) 37 DR 105

HOMEWORK

The law has very little to say on the subject of homework. Schools are under no statutory obligation to set homework although most do so, to a greater or lesser extent. Education authority schools must publish written information for parents about their policy on homework.

Most schools will set homework on a regular basis but the amounts, level and type of homework given will vary. HM Inspectorate of Education expects that homework will be set. It is seen as a way of improving the quality, range and appropriateness of teaching. Homework should be used effectively, be well planned and linked to classwork.

It is lawful for a school to make reasonable levels of homework a compulsory part of its school education. If school rules require pupils to complete homework, then a pupil can lawfully be subject to discipline for failing to complete homework set.

See also

Discipline and punishment
Information for parents

Useful organisations

Learning and Teaching Scotland
Parentzone

Useful publications

Scottish Executive (2004) *Homework: A guide for parents* (available from the Scottish Government)

Legal references used in this section

Schedule I, Part II (e) of the Education (Schools and Placing Information) (Scotland) Regulations 1982

HUMAN RIGHTS

The Convention for the Protection of Human Rights and Fundamental Freedoms was signed by the United Kingdom in 1950. Until 1999, it had no direct application in the United Kingdom, and the only way British citizens could access the rights it gave them was to take action in the Court of Human Rights in Strasbourg. This was a very lengthy process.

The Human Rights Act 1998 came into force on 2 October 2000, and has far reaching implications. The main changes it led to are:

• *Every public authority must act in accordance with human rights.* A "public authority" is any body that carries out functions of a public nature, and includes schools (except independent schools) and education authorities.

• *When courts are interpreting legislation, they must do so in a way which is compatible with human rights.* If they find that a piece of legislation is incompatible with human rights, they will issue a "declaration of incompatibility". This, however, does not invalidate a piece of Westminster legislation, it only draws Parliament's attention to the defect.

The Scottish Parliament is only allowed to make laws which comply with human rights. The Scottish Ministers have no powers to do anything which would be incompatible with human rights. Therefore, a court could strike down incompatible legislation, or parts of legislation from the Scottish Parliament, or incompatible acts by the Scottish Ministers.

The relevant human rights are:

The Convention for the Protection of Human Rights and Fundamental Freedoms:

Article 2:	Right to life
Article 3:	Prohibition of torture and inhuman or degrading treatment
Article 4:	Prohibition of slavery and forced labour
Article 5:	Right to liberty and security
Article 6:	Right to a fair trial
Article 7:	No punishment without law
Article 8:	Right to respect for family and private life
Article 9:	Freedom of thought, conscience and religion
Article 10:	Freedom of expression
Article 11:	Freedom of assembly and association
Article 12:	Right to marry
Article 14:	Prohibition of discrimination (in the application of Convention rights)
Article 16:	Restrictions on political activity of aliens
Article 17:	Prohibition of abuse of rights
Article 18:	Limitation on use of restrictions on rights

1st Protocol:

    1: Protection of property

    2: Right to education.
No person shall be denied the right to education. In the exercise of any functions which it assumes in relation to education and to teaching, the State shall respect the right of parents to ensure such education and teaching is in conformity with their own religious and philosophical convictions. (The UK Government has qualified this right, to say it only applies if it is compatible with the provision of efficient instruction and training and does not require unreasonable public expenditure.)

    3: Right to free elections

6th Protocol:

    1: Abolition of death penalty

    2: Death penalty in time of war

Human rights and education

The right to education in Protocol 1 is a very general right, and the provisions of the Education (Scotland) Act 1980 and the Standards in Scotland's Schools etc (Scotland) Act 2000 go well beyond what is required by this provision. Human rights issues have been raised in relation to various educational matters including: school uniform; corporal punishment; religious education; exclusion from school; placing requests: and the education of travellers. These are discussed in the relevant sections of this book

Educational decisions made by schools (except independent schools), education authorities, further and higher education institutions, grant-making bodies, education appeal committees, children's hearings and courts all have to conform with human rights.

A successful challenge to a decision which breached a pupil's (or parent's) human rights may lead to an award of damages.

If a pupil's human rights may have been breached by a public authority, legal advice should be sought as soon as possible. Any court action claiming a violation of human rights must begin within a year of the incident complained about.

If the domestic courts refuse a human rights claim, it is still possible to take cases to the European Court of Human Rights. Given the length of time such a case would take to be concluded, this may not be a particularly effective remedy.

Scottish Commission for Human Rights

The first Scottish Commission for Human Rights has been appointed and will begin operating in late 2008. The Commission has a general duty to promote human rights. In this context "human rights" means not just the rights from the European Convention, but human rights from any international treaty or convention ratified by the United Kingdom e.g. the UN Declaration of Human Rights.

The Commission has powers to review and recommend changes to the law of Scotland or the policies or practices of Scottish public authorities. The Commission can also conduct formal inquiries and intervene in civil court proceedings to give its views to the court on human rights issues raised in a case.

Useful organisations

Article 12
Equality and Human Rights Commission
European Court of Human Rights
Scotland's Commissioner for Children and Young People

Legal References

European Convention on Human Rights

Human Rights Act 1998

Scottish Commission for Human Rights Act 2006

INDEPENDENT SCHOOLS

Any parent is entitled to seek a place at an independent (or private) school for their child. Parents do not have to send their children to an education authority school provided they have made adequate alternative arrangements for their children's education. Admission to an independent school is usually handled by way of parental application. Prospective pupils may have to attend an interview and may have to sit a school entrance examination or test before being offered a place. This type of entrance exam for independent schools is a "permitted form of selection" in terms of the Disability Discrimination Act 1995. This means that it is not unlawful to refuse entry to an independent school based on academic ability.

Organisation and courses taught

Independent schools vary greatly in their character and size and in the range of pupils admitted. Some are different in their educational approach from others or have special interests like creative arts. Some provide schooling from age 5 or pre-school right through to school leaving age and beyond. Some take in boys or girls only, and some are mainly for boarders. A number cater exclusively for children with additional support needs / special educational needs or disabilities. Others cater specially for children with special abilities and aptitudes, for example in dance, drama and music. Most independent schools will offer a range of courses and subjects very similar to local authority schools, and enter pupils for the same examinations. Classes in independent schools are often smaller than those in education authority schools.

Registration of independent schools

Any person, group of people or organisation (including parents and parents' organisations) can set up a school. Any school (other than a local authority one) which offers full-time education for children of school age must be registered as an independent school. It is a criminal offence to run an unregistered school.

Anyone proposing to set up an independent school must apply to the Scottish Ministers to register that school. The application must contain specific information about the proposed school, as set out on regulations.

The Scottish Ministers may grant an application for registration provided that they are satisfied that:

- efficient and suitable instruction will be provided at the school, having regard to the ages and sex of the pupils who shall be attending the school;
- the welfare of such pupils will be adequately safeguarded and promoted;
- the proprietor of the school is a proper person to be the proprietor of an independent school;
- every proposed teacher in the school is a proper person to be a teacher in any school;
- the proposed school premises are suitable for use as a school; and
- the accommodation to be provided at the school premises is adequate and suitable, having regard to the number, ages and sex of the pupils who shall be attending the school.

The Scottish Ministers may grant an application for registration subject to conditions for carrying on the school.

Anyone who has been disqualified from working with children in terms of the Protection of Children (Scotland) Act 2003 is not a "proper person" to be a proprietor or teacher at an independent school.

A pre-registration visit will be carried out by HM Inspectorate of Education, who will tour the accommodation, interview the headteacher, speak informally to any other staff who may already be in post, and scrutinise any additional relevant documentation. They will then provide advice as to whether Ministers should register the school at this stage.

If an application for registration is refused, the Scottish Ministers may make an order disqualifying premises, accommodation, proposed proprietors or proposed teachers. This means that they could not have any future involvement in that or any other school.

There is a right of appeal against a decision to refuse registration, impose conditions or disqualify. The appeal must be made within 28 days and is heard by the Sheriff Principal.

If an application is successful, the Registrar of Independent Schools will enter the school's details in the register of independent schools. The register of independent schools is a public record and contains the name, address and proprietor of each independent school in Scotland. A copy of the register is available from the Scottish Government, through the Registrar. It is also available online at the Scottish Government's website in the near future. It is a criminal offence to run an independent school which is not registered.

Inspections

Independent schools, like education authority ones, are open to inspection at any time. Inspectors have to be satisfied that:

• efficient and adequate education is being provided for pupils there;
• the school is run and staffed by suitable people;
• the school's premises are suitable and the accommodation adequate; and
• the welfare of the pupils attending the school is adequately safeguarded and promoted.

Failure to meet these requirements could result in removal of the school from the register.

Complaints

Parents (or others) may at any time make a complaint to the Scottish Ministers about an independent school: for example, if the school were badly managed, or the children's welfare not looked after properly. Advice should be sought before making a complaint. If a complaint is accepted, the school could face removal from the register. The school can make an appeal about such a decision to the Sheriff Principal. If the complaint is about an individual teacher then that teacher must be named and notified of the complaint. The teacher would have the right of appeal in that case.

Parents' legal rights

Where a child attends a fee-paying school, the parent (or other fee-payer) is in a contractual relationship with the school. They have agreed to pay fees in exchange for educational services. Just as the school could sue for breach of contract if the fees were not met, so parents are able to sue the school for breach of contract where the services provided are deficient in some way. The terms and conditions and the prospectus of the school can be used to show what the school were offering to provide. Legal advice should be sought before considering such action.

See also

Inspections and inspectors' reports

Useful organisations

Scottish Council for Independent Schools
Scottish Government

Useful publications

Scottish Executive (2006) *The Registration of Independent Schools in Scotland: Guidance Notes* (available from the Scottish Government)

Legal references used in this section

Sections 30, 66, 98, 99, 100 et seq.; Education (Scotland) Act 1980

Registration of an Independent School (Scotland) Regulations 1957

Section 17; Protection of Children (Scotland) Act 2003

Part 2; School Education (Ministerial Powers and Independent Schools) (Scotland) Act 2004

Registration of Independent Schools (Scotland) Regulations 2006

INFORMATION FOR PARENTS

Getting to know about the school

Parents are entitled to receive written information about their children's school(s), if it is run by an education authority, on request or once offered a place there. The type of information to which parents are entitled is laid down by law, and falls into three categories:

• basic information;

• school information; and

• supplementary information.

Basic information

Basic information is intended mainly for parents thinking of choosing an alternative school for their child (other than the local school). This must include information about how the education authority goes about:

• offering school places to pupils, including priorities for admissions where placing request demand exceeds available spaces;

• arranging for the admission of pupils who have not reached school starting age; and

• providing school meals, transport and boarding accommodation.

For each school the basic information must cover its name, address, telephone number, approximate roll, stage(s) of education provided, denomination (if any) and the gender of pupils admitted.

The information must also include addresses and telephone numbers of education and divisional education offices and contact points for parents who want more information or who think that their child has additional support needs. Basic information does not have to include information about nursery schools or classes, although parents are entitled to such information on request.

School information

School information is intended for parents of children already attending or about to attend a particular school or who want to choose a school in another area. This information must cover:

- the name, address and telephone number of the school, its present roll, stages of education provided, denomination (if any) and the gender of pupils admitted;
- the name of the head teacher and the number of teaching staff. nursery schools or classes must also give the number of nursery nurses, and special schools must also give the number of specially qualified staff;
- arrangements for parents whose children are offered or are seeking a place at the school to visit it;
- the school's educational aims;
- details about the curriculum, including the school's policy on homework and the provision of religious education and observance and parents' rights in that regard. secondary schools must also mention the courses they provide, personal and careers guidance, and arrangements for parents to be consulted about school subject options and choices;
- the school's arrangements for assessing pupils' progress and making pupils' progress reports available to parents;
- out-of-school hours activities;
- school sports and outdoor activities and facilities available;
- the school's policy on uniform and clothes and the approximate cost of each item of required uniform;
- the school's policy on discipline, school rules, and the enforcement of attendance;

- arrangements for providing meals, including entitlement to free school meals and where to apply for them, also facilities for eating packed lunches;
- arrangements for medical care for pupils;
- organisation of the school day, including arrival and dismissal times, school term dates, and holidays for the forthcoming session; and
- (for primary schools) the name, address and telephone number of the school to which pupils will normally transfer when they go on to secondary education;

Secondary schools (other than special schools) must also:

- say how pupils are grouped into classes for different subjects (i.e. mixed ability, ability sets, split classes etc.);
- set out their policy on entering pupils for public examinations; and
- give the number of pupils passing exams conducted by the Scottish Qualifications Authority, including details of the year group and grades;

Special schools must provide information about what particular needs are catered for, and what specialist services are available.

Supplementary information

Supplementary information is intended for parents wanting additional information for a variety of reasons but which is not given out as a matter of course. Parents are entitled to receive on request supplementary information about:

- *school admission arrangements*: school catchment areas, names of "feeder" primary schools and "receiving" secondary schools, and where pupils normally go from schools which do not cover all stages of primary or secondary education;
- *choice of school*: parents' rights to request an alternative school, the circumstances in which such requests can be refused; parents' right to appeal; any guidelines issued by the education authority for admitting pupils to schools or nursery classes where placing request demand exceeds available places;

- *school rolls*: how the education authority decides the maximum number of pupils for each school or stage;
- *rights of parents and young people to appeal*: against certain decisions about additional support needs;
- *the education authority's policies and practices on*: what is taught, assessment and exams; pupils with special abilities; school meals; school clothing and uniform; bursaries, grants and other financial help; discipline and other school rules; pupils with additional support needs; and Parent Councils;
- *names of nursery schools and nursery classes*, with addresses, telephone numbers and approximate rolls;
- *names of special schools* not run by the education authority but to which they normally send pupils, including for each school the name address and telephone number, current roll, stages of education covered, the additional support needs catered for, and specialist services provided; and
- *names of schools in which Gaelic is taught.*

Where is this information found?

Basic information

The education authority must let parents see the basic information at any of their schools, main or divisional education offices and, if possible, public libraries in their area. This information only has to be about schools in that local area.

Parents are entitled to be sent the information free of charge if they live in the education authority area, if they are about to move to the area, or are considering sending their children to school there.

School information

The education authority must give parents a copy of the information about a particular school as soon as their child is offered a place there or on request. This will often be in the form of a school handbook or prospectus, and must be given free of charge. Parents are entitled to receive information about any number of schools run by the education authority (or by other education authorities).

Basic and School information

The basic and school information must be brought up to date annually and state which year it is for. It must also be published in Gaelic (in Gaelic speaking areas) or other languages, if necessary.

Supplementary information

The education authority must give parents any supplementary information they request if they live in or are to move to the area or are considering placing their child in a school there. The information can be given verbally or in writing, although the parent can insist that verbal information is confirmed in writing. Information about legal appeal rights must be confirmed in writing. A map of a school's catchment area must be available at each school and at the head or divisional education office.

Supplementary information may be available in places such as public libraries, but will also be found at each individual school (in relation to that school).

Annual Statement of Education Improvement Objectives

Each year the education authority must publish its objectives for improving education, within the current national priorities in education and performance indicators (as defined by the Scottish Ministers). It must consult with parents' groups (among others) when preparing the statement. It must include details of how the education authority will try to involve parents in promoting the education of their children. An annual report on its success (or otherwise) in meeting these objectives must also be prepared.

School Development Plan

Each year the education authority must prepare, for each of its schools, a school development plan. The development plan sets objectives for each school based on the annual statement of education improvement objectives. The development plan must be prepared after consultation with (among others) the Parent Council, and any other parents' groups for that school. Again an annual report must be prepared to show what has been done to put the plan into practice within the school.

Parents of pupils at the school are entitled to free access to the plan and the report on request (and to a free copy of a summary of the plan and/or report).

Review of School Performance

The education authority must, from time to time, assess the quality of each school's education against its own measures and standards for judging performance. Where a school fails to meet the standards, the education authority must take action to put right the problems.

When deciding the measures and standards of performance, the education authority must consult with parents' groups and others. The measures and standards must be published.

See also

Accessibility strategies
Additional Support for Learning
Appeals
Careers education
Choice of school (including placing requests)
Guidance

Useful organisations

Scottish Parent Council Association
Scottish Parent Teacher Association
Parentzone

Useful publications:

Scottish Executive (2005) *Sharing Information* (available from the Scottish Government)

Scottish Executive (2006) *Parents as Partners in their Children's Learning: Toolkit* (available from the Scottish Government)

Legal references used in this section

Sections 28I, 28J, 28K; Education (Scotland) Act 1980

Education (Schools and Placing Information) (Scotland) Regulations 1982

Sections 4,5,6 and 7; Standards in Scotland's Schools etc. Act 2000

INSPECTIONS AND INSPECTOR'S REPORTS

Her Majesty's Inspectorate of Education (generally known as HMIE) is part of the Scottish Government and has the power and the task of inspecting all schools and educational establishments in Scotland. This includes nurseries, primary, secondary and residential schools, further education establishments and education authorities. Parents will normally be told in advance that their children's school is to be inspected, although some types of inspection are carried out without notice.

There are currently 8 categories of inspection:

1. Pre-school inspections;
2. Primary school inspections;
3. Secondary school inspections;
4. College reviews;
5. Community learning and development inspections;
6. Teacher Education;
7. Inspection of the education functions of local authorities (INEA); and
8. Services for children inspections.

The inspection report will highlight what the school does well and where it needs to improve. It will answer the following questions.

• How well do children learn and achieve?

• Does the school have a clear sense of direction?

• How well do staff work with others to support children's learning?

• Are staff and children actively involved in their community?

• Does the school have high expectations of all children?

The inspection will be carried out by a small team of inspectors, Associate Assessors (AA) and a Lay Member (LM) working for HM Inspectorate of Education (HMIE). In very small schools, one HM Inspector (HMI) will inspect the school.

Parental input to inspections

parents seeking their views on the school and indicate their priorities so that HMIE can take their interests into account. Those parents who are not part of the random sample may request a questionnaire. Lay members of the inspection team may also telephone parents or hold meetings with parents as necessary. Similarly, the lay inspectors are likely to interview the chair of the parent council or other parents group. There is also provision for a random selection of pupils to take part in the survey and inspectors will meet with groups of pupils to ensure that their views are heard.

After an inspection

Following an inspection, HMIE will produce a report. A copy of this report will be sent to each parent with a child at the school. Within 4 months of the publication of the report, the school and the education authority will issue an action plan detailing how they will deal with any points raised in it. Usually, within around 2 years of the publication of the HMIE report, the Inspectors will carry out a follow up inspection to see how well the points in the action plan have been implemented.

Education authorities, as well as schools, can now be inspected to review the way in which they are exercising their functions as to the provision of school education. This can be a general inspection, or can look into specific aspects of the education authority's functions. The education authority must give all reasonable assistance to whomever is carrying out the inspection.

In addition to the inspection of individual schools, HMIE analyses the results of its inspections on a national level, in order to inform the Scottish Ministers and Scottish Government of the current and future educational issues to help them improve the quality of education throughout Scotland. Sometimes the Scottish Ministers or the Scottish Government will ask HMIE to carry out investigations into specific topics related to educational matters. HMIE also uses the expertise it has developed to provide professional advice on education to education providers and other bodies.

Care Commission

The Care Commission has responsibility for inspecting care provision for all sectors and ages. This includes care services for children in the voluntary, private, local authority and independent school sectors. HMIE and the Care Commission carry out joint inspections in pre-school education, school hostels, residential schools and boarding schools, as well as children's services in local authorities

Useful organisations

Care Commission
HM Inspectorate of Education

Useful publications

HM Inspectorate of Education (2007) *The Journey to Excellence*

Scottish Executive (2003) *National Care Standards – Early Education and Childcare up to the age of 16* (available from the Scottish Government)

Legal references used in this section

Sections 66, 66A; Education (Scotland) Act 1980

Regulation of Care (Scotland) Act 2001

LEAVING AGE

Parents are required to make sure that, as long as their children are of school age (whether they attend school or not), they provide efficient education for the children that is suitable to their age, abilities and aptitudes.

There are two school-leaving dates:

> Summer leaving date: this is 30 May. If a child reaches the age of 16 between 1 March and 30 September, he or she can leave school at the summer leaving date.

> Winter leaving date: this is the first day of the Christmas holidays (or, where a child is not being educated at a school, 21 December). If a child reaches the age of 16 between 1 October and 28 (or 29) February, he or she can leave school at the winter leaving date.

Although children are allowed to leave school once they reach school leaving age, they are also allowed to stay on at school.

Once a child reaches school leaving age, he or she is legally termed a "young person". A young person is anyone over school leaving age who has not attained the age of 18. Many of the legal rights of parents transfer to the young person at school leaving age (such as the right to make a placing request). In the case of pupils with additional support needs which mean that they are unable to exercise their rights as a "young person", the parents retain these rights even though their child has reached school leaving age.

See also

Careers education
Children's rights
Post-16 education and lifelong learning

Useful organisations

Careers Scotland
Enquire
Learn Direct Scotland
Parentzone

Useful publications

Enquire *Factsheet 16: Leaving School and Deciding What to Do at 16+*

Legal references used in this chapter

Sections 31, 33, 135; Education (Scotland) Act 1980

LEGAL ACTION

A last resort

While it is possible to take legal action, for example to make the education authority carry out its statutory duties, it is important to see such action very much as a last resort, only after attempts at an amicable solution have failed. Sometimes taking legal action can damage relations between parents and schools. Parents should consider carefully balancing what can be achieved by taking legal action against any negative effects on their child's education. It is also worthwhile bearing in mind that court actions can take some time (perhaps even years) to be completed, it can be costly and that there is never a guarantee of success.

Who can take legal action?

Where duties are owed to the parent (e.g. a duty to consult on school closure plans), any legal action can be raised in the parent's name. Where the legal duty is owed to the child (e.g. the right to school education), any action should be raised in his or her name. Any child who is able to understand what consulting a solicitor and raising a court action means can do so in his or her own right, without a parent's permission. There is a presumption that children aged 12 and over have this level of understanding. If a child is too young to consult a solicitor on his or her own, then his or her parent(s) can do so and raise court action on his or her behalf. Parents may also bring court action on behalf of their children under the age of 16, if the child prefers. Where the young person is over 16 but does not have legal capacity to raise court action, the parent (or someone else) would need to seek powers from the court to do so on the young person's behalf (e.g. an intervention order).

In the case of children attending independent schools, many of the rights depend on the contractual agreement between parent and school, rather than on statutory provisions or at common law. In this case, the parent, rather than the child, would be the one to raise any legal action. This applies even where the pupil is over the age of sixteen, because the parent is the one who has a contract with the school.

Do you need a solicitor to take legal action?

Parents (or pupils) do not *have* to employ a solicitor to take legal action, but it can be very difficult (in many cases virtually impossible) for people to successfully negotiate the legal maze unaided.

Different kinds of legal action

There are a number of different kinds of legal action which can be taken in relation to education matters. Some of the more common of these are:

Judicial review

This type of action can only be raised in the Court of Session in Edinburgh. It is a way of challenging a decision made by an education authority or other public body, where no other means of appeal is available. Judicial review would be appropriate if an education authority fails to fulfil a statutory duty (e.g. the duty to provide alternative education to a child who has been excluded from school) or if it has exercised its discretion unreasonably (e.g. in refusing to provide transport to school).

Appeals

The process for appeals is set out in the law. There are a number of different types of educational appeal, including exclusion appeals, placing request appeals, appeals relating to additional support needs, and appeals against the making of an attendance order. (see **Appeals** section for more details)

Compensation claims

If someone has been injured (physically, psychologically or financially) because of someone else's fault, negligence or failure to fulfil a statutory duty, then the injured person may be entitled to financial compensation. Examples of this could include a child being injured because of a lack of supervision within the school. It may also be possible to claim compensation for lack of educational attainment or employment prospects if an education authority has failed, for example, to provide appropriate educational provision for a child or has failed to tackle bullying effectively. Generally, in educational matters, the pursuer (i.e. the person bringing the case) has to prove that there was professional negligence in order to win the case. This type of case can be very difficult to prove, and parents (or pupils) will certainly need specialist advice and representation to take this type of action.

Interdict

This is a way of preventing the education authority or any other person doing something which it is not allowed to do. It is the Scots law equivalent of an injunction.

Human Rights issues

If an education authority (or other public body) has breached a pupil's (or parent's) Convention rights, then that breach can be raised as part of another relevant court action – as described above. Alternatively, the victim of the breach can raise a court action relying solely on the human rights argument. Compensation may be available where there has been a breach (see **Human rights** section for more information).

Action which can be taken against pupils or parents

There are also instances where action can be taken against parents or pupils. For example, parents may be prosecuted and/or children referred to a children's hearing in relation to any of the following:

- failure to attend school regularly, without reasonable excuse;
- failure to submit a child for assessment or examination for a record of needs; or
- failure to comply with the terms of an attendance order.

Local authorities may also seek to take legal action preventing an abusive or threatening parent from going near the school or school staff. If legal action is taken against a parent or pupil, legal advice should be sought as soon as possible.

Financing legal action

Funding may be available for legal advice and representation from the Scottish Legal Aid Board (SLAB). Eligibility will depend on the income and capital of the person receiving the advice or representation (which may be the child). A solicitor will be able to advise on whether someone is financially eligible for Legal Aid. Most children will be eligible under the financial criteria. SLAB offers two basic schemes:

- "Advice and Assistance" covers legal advice and assistance from a solicitor. It would cover things like a solicitor's letter to the school or education department and meeting with the solicitor to get some advice on a legal problem at school. Sometimes an increase in authorised expenditure can be granted to cover more expensive items e.g. where the solicitor has to enter into more prolonged correspondence on an issue or to pay for outlays such as a medical or psychological report. Depending on the person's income, there may be a contribution to make.

- "Legal Aid" covers legal representation in court and work associated with such court action. Legal aid is also available for some types of tribunal representation. It is not currently available for representation before the education appeal committee nor the Additional Support Needs Tribunals.

If you have a strong or deserving case, you may be able to find a solicitor who will act for you on an "no win no fee" basis or pro bono (for free). If there is a law centre which covers you area, the advice and representation they provide will usually be free. The

Equality and Human Rights Commission in Scotland will also fund some cases relating to discrimination law, where the outcome of the case may be of strategic importance.

See also

Advice and assistance
Appeals
Children's hearings
Complaints
Human rights

Useful organisations

Cl@nLaw
Govan Law Centre: Education Law Unit
Law Society of Scotland
Scottish Child Law Centre
Scottish Legal Aid Board

Useful publications

Consumer Focus Scotland (2008) *The Legal System in Scotland (Fourth Edition)* (available from TSO)

LOOKED AFTER CHILDREN

A large number of children and young people come to the attention of local social work services every year. This may be for a variety of reasons. For example, their parents may have difficulties in caring for them; they may be involved in offending or drug or alcohol misuse; or the children may not be attending school. Most of these children receive services from the local authority while they continue to live at home. Indeed, local authorities have an obligation to try to keep children at home with their parents or some other family member wherever possible.

In some cases however, children cannot be cared for by their parents and may be taken into care by the local authority. The law says these children are "'looked after and accommodated" by the local authority, and this gives the local authority additional responsibilities towards them. Children can be looked after away from home in a number of different settings – some may stay with relatives or foster carers, others may stay in children's homes or residential schools. Children placed in residential schools by the local authority, including those placed in independent and grant-aided special schools, may be regarded as looked after children, depending on the circumstances. The local authority has an obligation to try to find the most appropriate placement for each child it looks after.

There are a number of ways that a child can become looked after. A child is "looked after" by a local authority if:

• the authority is providing accommodation for them under section 25 of the Children (Scotland) Act 1995;

• they are subject to a supervision requirement from the Children's panel; or

- if there is an order, authorisation or warrant in place which effectively appoints the local authority to look after the child.

A child may be looked after by the local authority and still staying at home with his or her parent(s) or carer(s).

Where a child is looked after by a local authority the authority must:

- safeguard and promote the child's welfare (which must be the authority's paramount concern);
- make services available for children cared for by their own parents as they think reasonable;
- promote, on a regular basis, personal relations and direct contact between the child and their parent(s), where practicable and appropriate;
- provide advice and assistance to prepare the child for when he or she is no longer looked after by a local authority.

Before making any decision about a looked after child the local authority must, where practicable, ascertain and have regard to the views of—

- the child;
- their parents;
- anyone else with parental rights; and
- anyone else whose views the authority think are relevant.

They must also have regard to the child's religious persuasion, racial origin and cultural and linguistic background.

Voluntary care

Sometimes, parents ask for their children to be looked after by the local authority. This can be for a variety of reasons. Parents may have to spend some time in hospital and have no one who can care for their children while they are away. They may be unable or unwilling to care for their children. There is no maximum or minimum period that a child can remain looked after and accommodated on a voluntary basis. Some children have a programme of respite care where they regularly spend a couple of nights every week or month away from home on a planned basis.

Generally speaking, parents will be asked to sign a document agreeing to their children being looked after and accommodated by the local authority. Parents can ask for their children to be returned to their care at any time, but must give the local authority some notice of this. The amount of notice needed depends on the length of time the child has been away from home. If the local authority has received a parental request for a child to be returned, but feels it would not be in that child's best interests to return home, it may take steps to have the child remain looked after and accommodated by them on a compulsory basis.

Very occasionally, children themselves may ask to be looked after by the local authority.

Whenever children are looked after on a voluntary basis, their parents retain all of their parental rights. Parents must therefore be consulted, whenever decisions are being made, for example about a change of school or of placement.

Compulsory care

If the local authority believes it would be in a child's best interests to be looked after and accommodated by them, but the parents disagree, the authority can take steps to remove the child from his or her home. Authorisation for this can only be granted in very limited circumstances, for example if a child is at risk at home, or has committed offences or is misusing alcohol or drugs. In wholly exceptional cases, a child might be removed from their home as a result of a failure to attend school regularly.

In an emergency situation, e.g. where the local authority believes a child is at some immediate risk, it may apply to the court for a "child protection order." This gives authorisation for a child to be looked after and accommodated by the local authority for a short period until a children's hearing can be held to consider his/her case.

More commonly, authorisation for a child to be looked after and accommodated is given by a children's hearing. The children's hearing may issue a warrant which gives authorisation for a child to be looked after and accommodated by the local authority for periods of up to 22 days at a time, or may make a supervision requirement which applies for up to one year (see **Children's hearing** section for more information).

Even if a child is looked after and accommodated by the local authority on a compulsory basis, the child's parent(s) retain all of their parental rights in relation to education matters.

Getting it right for every child

"Getting It Right For Every Child" (affectionately known as "GIRFEC") was a consultation document published in 2005, principally concerned with reforming the children's support system in Scotland. Within that approach, an Integrated Assessment Framework (IAF) was designed to be a framework for action, which makes inter-agency assessment and planning effective.

A draft Children Services (Scotland) Bill has been produced, but it has not yet been enacted – nor are there any immediate plans to introduce the Bill to the Scottish Parliament. Therefore, GIRFEC has no statutory basis. Nevertheless, local authorities (and particularly local authority social work and education departments) do use the GIRFEC framework to inform the way in which they carry out their statutory functions.

The key principles behind the Integrated Assessment Framework are:

- it applies to all children (whether they are looked after or not);
- it aims to serve the best interests of the child or young person;
- it seeks to identify the earliest, most effective and least intrusive response to needs;

- it takes account of the views of the child or young person and the views of the family;
- it takes account of all aspects of the child's life, including any communication, cultural or religious needs in order to prevent discrimination; and
- it brings together professionals from different fields to work to make sure that assessments focus on
  - personal and family strengths,
  - support networks and resources available,
  - needs and risks,
  - the gaps that need to be filled and the resources and options to fill them, and
  - continuity and progression, especially at times of transition.

Getting it right for every child proposes that for all children who require one, there will be an integrated and agreed plan. The plan will be based on a view of the child's needs as a whole, identifying the action necessary to address those needs, specifying who is to take what action and recording what improved outcomes are expected within what timescale.

The Scottish Government's target was that every child going to a Children's Hearing should have such a plan by December 2007 with the following key features recorded:

- A summary of the needs which have to be addressed;
- What is to be done?;
- Who is to do it?;
- How will we know if there are improvements?; and
- Contingencies.

Assumption of parental rights

In very limited and exceptional cases, the local authority can take court action to assume parental rights over looked after children. If it is successful, the child's natural parents lose all of their parental responsibilities and rights to the local authority. This means that it is the local authority who then makes decisions about the child's education, not the natural parents.

Where a child is accommodated by a local authority in terms of the Children (Scotland) Act 1995, they are automatically said to be looked after by the local authority. However, where the accommodation is provided because of a placing request to a residential school, or because the education department have placed a child at a residential school because it can best meet that child's educational needs, then that child is accommodated in terms of the Education (Additional Support for Learning) (Scotland) Act 2004 and is not necessarily regarded as "looked after".

Children leaving care

If a child is looked after when he or she reaches school leaving age, then the local authority has powers to pay him or her a grant or make a contribution towards their accommodation and maintenance expenses while they are still in education or employment, or are seeking employment. Local authorities are also obliged to provide other support.

See also

Additional Support for Learning
Children's hearings

Useful organisations

Scottish Government
Scottish Throughcare & Aftercare Forum

Useful publications

Asquith, Stewart (Ed) (1995) *The Kilbrandon Report: Children And Young Persons Scotland* (available on the Children's Hearings website www.childrens-hearings.co.uk)

Scottish Executive (2007) *Getting it right for every child: Guidance on the Child's or Young Person's Plan* (available from the Scottish Government)

Scottish Government (2007) *Getting it right for every child in kinship and foster care*

Scottish Government (2008) *Getting it right for every child: Guidance on Overnight Stay for Looked After and Accommodated Children*

Scottish Government (2008) *Getting it right for children and young people who present a risk of serious harm: Meeting Need, Managing Risk and Achieving Outcomes*

Legal references used in this section

Part 2; Children (Scotland) Act 1995

MEDIATION

Mediation

The education authority must make appropriate arrangements to provide "independent" mediation services for the purposes of resolving disputes between parents or young people and the authority in relation to additional support needs and co-ordinated support plans (CSP).

Mediation is a form of assisted negotiation in which an independent third party helps the parties in dispute to reach a mutually acceptable outcome. It can be used in any circumstance where there is a disagreement related to a child or young person's additional support needs or CSP.

Mediation services may be provided by the education authority directly or by an outside agency, but the mediator cannot have any involvement with the education authority's functions which are related to additional support needs (other than mediation).

Neither the parent (or young person) nor the authority are obliged to agree to participate in mediation. The parent or young person must not be charged any fee for taking part. Involvement in mediation does not affect any entitlement to make a reference to the Additional Support Needs Tribunals.

See also

Additional Support for Learning
Complaints
Coordinated Support Plans
Dispute resolution

Useful organisations

Common Group Mediation
Enquire
Independent Special Education Advice (Scotland)
Parentzone
Resolve: ASL

Useful publications

Enquire *Factsheet 9: Mediation*

Education Law Unit: Govan Law Centre (2004) *Additional Support Needs Mediation: Setting up and delivering mediation services in the Scottish education system*

Legal references used in this section

Section 15 of the Education (Additional Support for Learning) (Scotland) Act 2004

MEDICAL ATTENTION

As a general rule, only those people with parental responsibilities for a child can consent (or withhold consent) to medical treatment or attention for their child. Those with parental rights include:

- mothers;
- fathers who are or have been married to the child's mother;
- fathers who have entered into a parental rights agreement with the child's mother;
- unmarried fathers (or others) who have acquired parental rights and responsibilities by court order; and
- (As of 4 May 2006) Fathers who are not married to the mother but are registered as the child's father at the registration of birth.

In emergency situations, someone over 16 who has care and control of a child but has no parental rights or responsibilities in relation to the child may consent to medical treatment on their behalf. This decision needs to be reasonable to safeguard the child's health, development and welfare and the person giving consent must have no reason to believe the parent(s) would refuse consent. This does not apply to teachers or others at school but would cover, for example grandparents who look after a child. On enrolling a child at school, parents will normally be asked for emergency contact numbers and these will be kept with the child's school record. In a case of real emergency – a life or death situation – a doctor will be able to carry out lifesaving treatment on a child even if there is no-one present who is able to consent to the treatment.

Children who have legal capacity to do so may consent (or refuse to consent) to surgical, medical or dental procedure or treatment. A child has legal capacity if, in the opinion of a medical practitioner attending on the child, the child has sufficient understanding of the procedure or treatment and its potential consequences. Children aged twelve and over are presumed to have legal capacity.

In school, medical or dental treatment, inspection or examination can only be carried out if the child (with legal capacity) consents. If a child does not have legal capacity, their parent's consent is needed.

Administration of Medicine

Scottish Government guidance on the administration of medicine in schools says that there should be a joint agreement between the Health Board and education authority covering a range of issues including the administration of medicines in school. In addition, every school's health and safety policy should include procedures for supporting pupils with health care needs (including administration of medicines). The education authority should have good practice guidelines to help schools draft their own policies.

Staff who administer medication for pupils are often doing so on a voluntary basis. Head teachers should allow staff to administer medication for pupils where they volunteer to do so, and provide support and training where necessary. Indeed, a failure to do so may amount to unlawful disability discrimination, because allowing staff to volunteer to administer medication for disabled pupils is likely to be a "reasonable step" the school have a duty to take (see **Disability discrimination**). Staff who are administering medication should receive proper training and guidance from health care professionals.

A pupil who requires help with medication at school should have an individual health care plan, which should be tailored to the pupil's individual needs. The plan should identify the level and type of support needed by the pupil at school. The following people should be involved in drawing up a plan:

• the relevant health care professional;
• the head teacher;

- the parent;
- the pupil (if the pupil has legal capacity);
- the class teacher, form teacher or guidance teacher;
- any care assistant or support staff who work with the pupil;
- the member(s) of staff who will be administering the medication;

And sometimes …

- a social worker; or
- a representative of a relevant voluntary organisation.

If children are going on a school trip their parents will be asked to sign a consent form in case their child requires medical treatment. Staff supervising school trips should be made aware of any medical needs, and any relevant emergency procedures. Sometimes an additional supervisor or parent may be required to accompany a particular pupil.

Useful organisations

Enquire
Equalities and Human Rights Commission
Independent Special Education Advice (Scotland)
Parentzone

Useful publications

British Institute of Learning Disability (2004) *Easy Guide to Being Held Safely* (available from www.bild.org.uk)

Scottish Executive (2001) *Administration of medicines in schools* (available from the Scottish Government)

Scottish Office (1999) *Helping Hands: guidelines for staff who provide intimate care for children and young people with disabilities* (available from the Scottish Government)

Legal references used in this section

Section 131A; Education (Scotland) Act 1980

Section 2(4); Age of Legal Capacity (Scotland) Act 1991

Sections 1, 5, 11; Children (Scotland) Act 1995

Section 23 of the Family Law (Scotland) Act 2006

PARENTAL INVOLVEMENT AND REPRESENTATION

Promoting involvement of parents in schools

The Scottish Ministers have a duty to promote the involvement of parents in the education of their children in schools. The education authority have a similar duty to promote parental involvement in the child's education and the education of children at the same school generally.

Every education authority must prepare a strategy for parental involvement which contains their general policies for parental involvement, parental involvement for looked after children and the complaints procedure. In preparing the strategy the authority must have regard to how it will promote equal opportunities.

The authority must review and revise their strategy from time to time as appropriate and in developing or reviewing their strategy they must seek and have regard to the views of parents, pupils, Parent Councils, and others with an interest in parental involvement.

The strategy must be included as part of the authority's annual statement of improvement objectives. Each school's development plan must include objectives for parental involvement.

In reviewing the quality of education provided by a school, the education authority must take into account the extent to which parents are involved in their children's education.

Parent Forums and Parent Councils

The parents of pupils at an authority school are collectively known as the Parent Forum of that school. A Parent Forum may be represented by establishing a Parent Council. The education authority are obliged to promote the establishment of Parent Councils and to support their operation.

A Parent Council is an independent organisation with a constitution (a copy of which must be provided to both the education authority and the head teacher). A Parent Council is called "[name of school] Parent Council" unless the Parent Forum decides otherwise.

Parent Council: members and chair

Members of a Parent Council must be parents of pupils at the school or (where the constitution allows) co-opted members. For denominational schools, the Parent Council's constitution must provide for at least one of the co-opted members to be nominated by the church or denominational body in question.

The chair of a Parent Council must be the parent of a pupil at the school.

Parent Council: functions

The functions of a Parent Council are–

(a) to support the school in –

  (i) raising standards of education at the school,

  (ii) improving the quality of education at the school, and

  (iii) developing to their fullest potential the personality, talents and mental and physical abilities of pupils attending the school,

(b) to make representations–

  (i) to the school's headteacher and to the education authority about the school's arrangements for promoting parental involvement,

  (ii) to the education authority about the authority's arrangements for promoting parental involvement,

(c) to promote contact between–

(i) the school,

(ii) the Parent Forum,

(iii) parents of prospective pupils of the school,

(iv) pupils at the school,

(v) the community, and

(vi) other appropriate people or bodies,

(d) to report on the Parent Council's activities to the other parents at the school at least once every 12 months.

(e) to canvas the views of the parents at the school on–

(i) the standards of education in the school,

(ii) the quality of education at the school,

(iii) the Parent Council, and

(iv) other matters of interest or concern to the parents,

(f) to collate those views and report them to–

(i) the headteacher of the school,

(ii) the education authority, and

(iii) other appropriate people or bodies.

The Parent Council of any primary school should promote contact between parents of pupils at the school, and nursery education providers whose children may be prospective pupils of the school.

The Parent Council may make representations on any matter to–

(a) the headteacher of the school,

(b) the education authority, or

(c) other appropriate people or bodies.

If a Parent Council plans to make representations to Her Majesty's Inspectorate of Education (other than in the course of an inspection) the Parent Council they must first have made the same representations to the authority and (except where it would be inappropriate to do so) to the headteacher and have received a response from both of them.

Having done so, where HMIE receive representations from a Parent Council they must have regard to those representations and must reply.

The Parent Council have a general power to do anything which help them to perform their functions. However, they may not entering into a contract or agreements in relation to land, nor may they make payments (other than out of pocket expenses) to any member of the council.

The Parent Council must comply with any reasonable request by the headteacher or the education authority for information relating to its functions.

Parent Council : meetings

The headteacher has both the duty and the right to attend, or (at the headteacher's discretion) to be represented at any meeting of a Parent Council. Only if the headteacher and the Parent Council agree can this requirement be dispensed with.

Meetings of a Parent Council are open to the public unless dealing with confidential matters.

Parent Council : financial powers

A Parent Council may raise funds by any means (other than borrowing money) and may spend any of its funds at its discretion (in accordance with the purposes of the council as set out in the constitution and in law).

A Parent Council must keep proper accounts, but it may not acquire any heritable property (land, buildings etc.) by any means. Where a Parent Council ceases to exist, any funds or other property belonging to it passes to the education authority; but the authority is to use any such property for the benefit of the school.

Duties to a Parent Council

The education authority must give advice and information to a Parent Council on any matter, if asked to do so. The headteacher of a school must give advice to the Parent Council on any matter falling within the headteacher's area of responsibility, if asked to do so.

In addition, the headteacher and school staff should be available to give advice and information to the Parent Council on what is being done to promote parental involvement at the school.

The education authority must provide a reasonable annual budget to each Parent Council to cover its administrative expenses, the costs of training its members, and any other relevant outgoings. The authority may also provide a Parent Council with services or accommodation.

If an education authority or headteacher receive representations from a Parent Council, they must have regard to those representations and reply to the council.

Duties to parents generally

The education authority must give advice and information to any parent of a pupil in their schools on any matter relating to the pupil's education, if asked to do so. Headteachers and school staff should also be available to give such advice and information to parents.

Parent Council : appointment of senior staff

Each education authority's appointment process for headteachers or deputy headteachers must include the involvement of the school's Parent Council (if any).

A Parent Council may ask a non-member to help it in the appointment process. The authority must make appropriate training available for members of the Parent Council and any person assisting them (as above).

Education authorities must involve the Parent Council in specified stages of the appointment process.

The authority must consult with the Parent Council, when preparing their recruitment strategies, and job or person specifications.

The education authority must invite the Parent Council to participate in preparing a short leet of candidates for the post. Where a Parent Council decides that it wishes to participate in the short leet procedure it will nominate one of its members (or the person who is assisting them with the appointment process) to do so. This does not apply where, following consultation, the education authority decides instead to fill a post by means of redeploying an existing headteacher or deputy headteacher currently employed elsewhere. In that case the Parent Council has no further involvement in the appointment process.

If the post is not to be filled by redeployment, then an appointment panel, to consider the short leet of candidates, and to make recommendations to the authority for appointment. The authority must invite the Parent Council to be represented on the appointment panel. If a Parent Council decides that it wishes to be represented on the appointment panel, at least one third of the panel must be members of the Parent Council or their nominated assistant (as before). The appointment panel will usually interview the candidates.

For the appointment of a headteacher, the appointment panel will be chaired by a person nominated by the education authority. For the appointment of a deputy headteacher, the appointment panel will be chaired by the headteacher or the acting headteacher of the school. The chair of an appointment panel shall have a casting vote on the recommendations to be made to the authority.

Setting up a Parent Council

If a school does not already have one, the legislation does not specify clearly how Parent Councils are to be established other than on commencement of the legislation.

Parents who wish to set up a Parent Council should contact their education authority. There should either be an existing scheme for the establishment of a Parent Council, or the authority should be asked to prepare a fresh scheme. Alternatively, the parents may wish to prepare a scheme themselves. Either way, the scheme must include the preparation of a constitution.

Every parent in the school should then be asked whether the scheme should be implemented. If a majority of parents responding agree that it should be, then the person who prepared the scheme may go ahead an implement it, bringing the new Parent Council into existence.

Other Parent Groups

Another way in which parents can become involved in what's going on at their child's school is through a Parent-Teacher Association (PTA) or a Parents' Association (PA). Generally there is little difference between the two, although as the name suggests, a PTA will tend to have teachers as members as well as parents. There is no legal requirement (or specific legal provision) for PTAs or PAs to be set up within schools, although some education authorities do encourage this.

Many PTAs or Pas have now simply become part of a Parent Council. However, there is nothing to stop parents from continuing or setting up a parent group which is not part of the Parent Council.

PTAs and PAs can become involved in a wide range of activities. Many are devoted solely to fundraising activities, while others take an active interest in educational and other matters affecting the school.

It is advisable to have a formal document or "constitution" setting out the aims of the association, how often meetings are held, how office bearers are appointed, etc. This is particularly the case if the association will be handling any money. Unlike Parent Councils, PTAs and PAs are liable for their actions, with members of their committees carrying any liability personally. The Scottish Parent Teacher Council gives advice to PTAs and PAs on, among other things, how to set up an association and insurance.

If a school does not have a PTA or PA, it is open to any parent to go about setting one up. The initial steps would be first to establish whether there is a willingness among other parents to become involved, and second to approach the Parent Council (if there is one) and the head teacher to see if they would be agreeable to setting one up. The permission of the Parent Council or headteacher is not required to set up a parent's group, but if either is opposed to it, it may be more difficult to fulfil certain functions. As the headteacher, the authority and the Parent Council are requirement to promote parental involvement, there is unlikely to be significant opposition to setting up a new group.

Many schools allow their PTAs or PAs to meet on school premises free of charge. However, they are not obliged to do so, and could charge for accommodation or even not allow the association to use school premises at all.

See also

Consulting parents
Information for parents

Useful organisations

Parentzone
Scottish Parent Council Association
Scottish Parent Teachers Council

Useful publications

Scottish Executive (2006) *Making the Difference: A new law to support parents* (available from the Scottish Government)

Scottish Executive (2006) *Parents as Partners in their Children's Learning: Toolkit* (available from the Scottish Government)

Scottish Executive (2006) *Guidance on the Scottish Schools (Parental Involvement) Act 2006* (available from the Scottish Government)

Scottish Government (2007) *Parent Council Welcome Pack*

Scottish Government (2007) *Scottish Schools (Parental Involvement) Act 2006: Guidance on Parental Involvement in the Appointment Processes for Headteacher and Deputy Headteacher Posts*

Scottish Government (2007) *Issues and Options for the Formation of a National Parent Body in Scotland*

Legal references used in this section

Scottish Schools (Parental Involvement) Act 2006

Parental Involvement in Headteacher and Deputy Headteacher Appointments (Scotland) Regulations 2007

Sections 5, 6; Standards in Scotland's Schools etc. (Scotland) Act 2000

PHYSICAL INTERVENTION AND RESTRAINT

Corporal punishment in schools is unlawful. School staff who inflict physical punishment on pupils are guilty of a criminal offence (assault) and would be liable in damages for any injuries caused. However, not all physical contact with pupils counts as corporal punishment.

The law envisages certain circumstances where physical contact on pupils by members of staff may be legitimate:

- to prevent an injury to the pupil;
- to prevent injury to someone else; or
- to prevent damage to property.

These circumstances broadly coincide with defences available to a charge of assault, provided that only reasonable force is used. It may sometimes be necessary to restrain a child for safety reasons e.g. in separating two pupils who are fighting, or in grabbing a child who is about to run onto a busy road. Pupils with some types of disability or with social, emotional and behavioural difficulties may require to be restrained more often than other children.

There is little guidance available to schools in Scotland about physical intervention and restraint. The guidance that is available states that:

- the main intention of restraint in any situation is to protect a child from harm, and should only be attempted as a last resort and when it can be achieved without causing harm to the child or to the member of staff involved;
- assistance from other staff, while preferable, may not always be possible;

- all incidents of restraint should be logged, dated and signed in a log kept for that purpose, and this log should be monitored by a member of the senior management team.

In settings where staff may require to physically restrain pupils on a regular basis:

- staff should receive specialised training for this role with regular refreshers;
- where individual pupils are known to require restraint, an individual plan or protocol should be drawn up, explaining precisely what action staff will take, and recording triggers, times and outcomes of incidents;
- the plan / protocol should be agreed with parents/carers (and, if appropriate, the child or young person);
- even for trained staff, restraint should only be used as a last resort.

In schools where there is likely to be a frequent need for restraint of pupils, these considerations may give rise to a duty to train staff. If a failure to train staff leads to injuries being sustained (by staff or pupils), the education authority or school proprietor may be liable in damages. Where properly trained staff use excessive force or inappropriate restraint techniques, this may lead to disciplinary measures being taken against them, or even dismissal.

See also

Additional Support for Learning
Discipline and punishment
Legal action
Safety and supervision

Useful organisations

Enquire
Independent Special Education Advice (Scotland)
Parentzone

Useful publications

Allen, D (Ed) (2002) *Ethical Approaches to Physical Intervention (available through the British Institute for Learning Disability www.bild.org.uk)*

Bell, L. And Stark, C. (1998) *Measuring Competence in Physical Restraint Skills in Residential Child Care: Social Work Research Findings No. 21* (available from the Scottish Govermnent)

Scottish Executive (2005) *Safe and well: Good practice in schools and education authorities for keeping children safe and well* (available from the Scottish Government)

Legal references used in this section

Section 16; Standards in Scotland's Schools etc. Act 2000

Judith McLeod v. Aberdeen City Council, 11 June 1999 Court of Session (Outer House)

Mary McLatchie v. Scottish Society for Autism, 4 February 2004 Court of Session (Outer House)

Andrew Porter v. Oakbank School, 19 March 2004 Court of Session (Inner House)

POST-16 EDUCATION AND LIFELONG LEARNING

Once pupils reach school leaving age, they are free to choose whether to stay on at school, go on to further education, take up a training place find employment etc.

Staying on at school

Pupils can generally stay on at local authority schools beyond their school leaving age, usually up to the age of 18, but sometimes longer (especially for pupils with additional support needs). There is no obligation on an authority to provide education beyond a young person's eighteenth birthday, though they are free to do so, and must exercise this discretion reasonably. Educational Maintenance Allowances (EMAs) are available for eligible pupils in fifth and sixth year (see **Financial assistance**).

Further and higher education

Education authorities can establish further education colleges within their area, and there are a number of independent colleges across Scotland. Further education colleges offer a wide range of courses, from recreational ones to courses which lead to formal qualifications. While good exam results are needed to get on some of the courses on offer, many have no formal entry requirements. There is an increasing emphasis on "lifelong learning", encouraging adults to continue learning long after they are of school leaving age. In addition to full time attendance, many courses are offered on a part-time, evening or flexible basis. There are also an increasing number of distance learning and internet based courses available. For many full time courses, financial assistance by way of bursaries or loans may be available, and students with children or other dependents may be eligible for additional assistance. Those considering taking up a college course should contact the college in the first instance to find out what type of financial assistance may be available.

Right to time off for education and training

Anyone aged 16-17 who is in employment and has not achieved a certain number of qualifications (see **Examinations and assessments**) has the right to a reasonable amount of paid time off work to study or train for a relevant qualification.

Additional Support Needs

Children and young people with additional support needs are subject to a specific transition process (see **Additional Support for Learning**).

See also

Additional Support for Learning
Careers education
Financial assistance

Useful organisations

Careers Scotland
Educational Maintenance Allowance Scotland
Enquire
Learn Direct Scotland
Parentzone
Universities and Colleges Admissions Service (UCAS)

Useful publications

Enquire *Factsheet 16: Leaving School and Deciding what to do at 16+*

Scottish Government (2008) *Helping You Meet the Cost of Learning: Asylum Seekers, Refugees, Migrant Workers and Non-UK EU Nationals: A Guide to Funding 2008-09 - for Practitioners Giving Advice*

Scottish Government (current edition) *Helping you meet the costs of learning: Part-time study*

Scottish Government (current edition) *Helping you meet the costs of learning: Information for new Higher Education Scottish students choosing to study in England, Wales or Northern Ireland 2006 - 2007*

Scottish Government (current edition) *Helping you meet the costs of learning: What Support is Available for Mature Scottish Students in Higher Education*

Scottish Government (current edition) *Helping you meet the costs of learning: What Support is Available for Young Scottish Students in Higher Education*

Legal reference used in this section

Sections 1, 65B, 65C, Education (Scotland) Act 1980

Further and Higher Education (Scotland) Act 1992

Sections 12, 13, Education (Additional Support for Learning) (Scotland) Act 2004

PRE-SCHOOL EDUCATION

Education authorities have an obligation to provide free pre-school education to "prescribed pre-school" children. Broadly, this means three and four year olds who are not yet old enough to start primary school. The starting point for free pre-school education depends on when the child's third birthday falls:

- between 1 March and 31 August, in the following autumn term;
- between 1 September and 31 December, in the following spring term;
- between 1 January and 28/29 February, in the following summer term.

Free pre-school education can be extended where parents of children with birthdays in January or February choose to defer their child's entry to primary school. In these cases, local authorities are required to provide an additional free year. Children with September to December birthdays will only be able to access an extra year at the discretion of their local authorities.

Prescribed pre-school children are entitled to a total of 475 hours of free pre-school education per annum (pro rata), which is 12.5 hours a week during the school term. Local authorities differ in whether this allocation must be taken as five 2.5 hour sessions a week or whether other, more flexible, approaches can be taken depending on families' needs. Scottish Government guidance encourage a more flexible approach. The education authority are allowed to charge fees for pre-school education which is provided to children who do not fall within the specified age-range, or is provided over and above the 475 hours a year.

Statutory pre-school education can be provided in local authority nurseries or schools, or in voluntary and private establishments that have pre-school education partnering arrangements with the local authority.

Do children have to go to attend pre-school education?

No, parents do not have to send their children to nursery or to pre-school education.

However, if there were concerns about the level of care a child was receiving at home, the social work department and/or other professionals may advise parents that their child's needs would be best met by taking up a nursery place (either a pre-school education place or a nursery place). In exceptional cases, if the parents ignored this advice, that might form part of the grounds for referral to a children's hearing on the basis of a lack of parental care or neglect. It would be open to the children's hearing, if they felt it was in the child's best interests, to attach a condition to any supervision requirement that he or she attend nursery education regularly. If such a condition was in place, then the parents would be required to send the child to nursery, and the case could be brought back to the children's hearing quickly for reconsideration if they did not comply. (see **Children's hearings**)

Is there a choice of pre-school places?

Parents are of course free to choose whatever nursery place they want, subject to availability, cost etc. The education authority, however, have discretion to allocate free pre-school education places as they wish. There is no right to make a placing request for a pre-school place, unless the child has additional support needs (see **Additional Support for Learning**).

Transport

If a child is receiving pre-school education from the education authority (whether or not a fee is paid), the authority may provide transport. There is no legal obligation for them to do so. If a nursery provision is named as the school to be attended in a child's Co-ordinated Support Plan, the education authority may have to provide transport (see **Coordinated Support Plan**).

Curriculum

There is a curriculum framework for children attending pre-school education places funded by the education authority. This 3 to 5 curriculum was developed by the Scottish Government and highlights the importance of play in young children's learning. When introduced, the Curriculum for Excellence will cover all children in education, from ages 3 to 18 (see **Curriculum – what is taught?**).

Inspection

Pre-school education providers will be jointly inspected by both the Care Commission and HM Inspectorate of Education.

Additional Support Needs

"Prescribed pre-school" children are covered by the Additional Support for Learning legislation (see section on **Additional Support for Learning**). This means that if a prescribed pre-school child (i.e. one who is receiving free nursery education, as above) has additional support needs, the education authority will have duties to that child, including a duty to make adequate and efficient provision for their needs.

Some other pre-school children (e.g. children under the age of three or deferring entry to school) will be covered by the Act, but only where the child has additional support needs arising from a disability (see section on Disability Discrimination) and they have been referred to the education authority by the Health Board.

See also

Additional Support for Learning
Admission to school
Children's hearings
Disability Discrimination
Inspections and inspector's reports
School starting age

Useful organisations

Care Commission
Enquire
Parentzone

Useful publications

Scottish Executive (2003) *National Care Standards – Early Education and Childcare up to the age of 16* (available from the Scottish Government)

Scottish Government (2008) *Final report from the workforce task group for the early years framework*

Legal references used in this section

Sections 32 to 37; Standards in Scotland's Schools etc. Act 2000

Provision of School Education for Children under School Age (Prescribed Children) (Scotland) Order 2002

Provision of School Education for Children under School Age (Prescribed Children) (Scotland) Amendment Order 2007

Sections 5(2) & (3), 29(3), Education (Additional Support for Learning) (Scotland) Act 2004

PROPERTY LOSS AND DAMAGE

Who is responsible for taking care of pupils' personal belongings?

Pupils are primarily responsible for taking reasonable care of any personal belongings they bring into school. Depending on children's age, parents should exercise an element of care and control over what their children bring to school.

Where the school has taken items of property into its safekeeping, then it must take reasonable care of those items and may be liable in compensation if they are damaged or stolen. This could include:

• coats and bags left in cloakrooms;
• valuables entrusted with teachers during physical education; or
• bicycles left in a designated area within the school.

The school also has duties not to cause damage or loss to pupils' property by its own negligence (or that of its employees). For example, if a chemistry demonstration was improperly supervised and a child's jumper was burned or stained, the child or their parents might have a claim against the school.

What are children allowed to take into school?

The school can specify in its school rules what sort of personal property may or may not be brought into school or lessons. Pupils may risk being disciplined for bringing prohibited items into school. Obvious examples would be cigarettes, alcohol, illegal drugs, or weapons.

Schools may also forbid or confiscate items which may interfere with schoolwork, such as handheld games consoles, camera phones, MP3 players or football stickers. Articles taken away from pupils must be returned when the child leaves the school premises. Not to do so could count as theft. The school may hand over to the police any illegal items.

Is there a claim for loss or damage?

Parents may be able to make a claim on their own household insurance for loss or damage to their children's property, depending on the terms of the insurance policy. Where the school can be shown to be at fault, parents or pupils should be able to claim against the education authority (or proprietor in the case of an independent school). However, just because something is damaged at school does not necessarily mean that the school is to blame. Parents may have to seek legal advice on bringing court action in cases of more valuable property.

What about damage to the school's property?

Pupils at school are often given text books and other items which belong to the school. Some reasonable wear and tear is to be expected (especially where younger children are concerned). Where a child has damaged, destroyed or lost school property either on purpose or through their own negligence, they (or their parents) may be asked to pay to have the item replaced.

See also

Discipline and punishment
Legal action

PUPILS' EDUCATIONAL RECORDS

Will records be kept about pupils?

A progress record must be kept for every child who attends a local authority school. This record can only be used for supervising the child's educational development and for giving advice and assistance to, or about, the child. This means that it should not ordinarily be shown to people like employers, social workers, or the police. The record is confidential and may only be disclosed to certain specified people.

What information is in the progress record?

The progress record must have the following information:

- The name and address of both pupil and parent(s);
- An alternative emergency contact;
- Any previous schools the pupil has attended;
- The dates and results of any objective, diagnostic, psychological or aptitude tests;
- The pupil's Co-ordinated Support Plan (if there is one);
- Anything which might hinder the pupil's educational abilities or attainment;
- The pupil's health record;
- Information about the pupil's emotional and social development (including, where appropriate, relationships with other pupils or teachers);
- The pupil's yearly educational progress report; and
- For secondary school pupils, details of any posts of responsibility held in school or other related organisations.

What happens when a child changes or leaves school?

If a child changes schools, the progress record must be transferred to the child's new school, if the school requests it. The education authority has to keep a progress report for at least five years after a pupil has left school.

Pupils' educational records

Educational records are records of information held by the education authority (or by an independent or grant-aided school) which relate to the school education of a pupil or former pupil and have been written or created by:

• a teacher or other school or education authority employee; or
• the pupil or the pupil's parent.

Information contained in a Co-ordinated Support Plan does not fall under the heading of "educational records" and is dealt with under separate rules (see below). Information which is kept by a teacher about a pupil solely for the teacher's own use is also exempt from the category of "educational records". However, such information may be covered by the Data Protection Act (see below).

Parents can make a request for disclosure of their child's educational records. Parents can request either that the records be made available for inspection or that a copy be provided (on payment of an appropriate fee, which must not exceed the equivalent fee under the Data Protection Act). In making the request parents must supply enough information to prove that they are who they say they are and to specify what information they are looking for. Disclosure must be made within 15 school days of the request.

A request for disclosure can be made in writing, by email or in another permanent form. If the information from a child's educational records is required in an alternative language or format, then this must be supplied (at no extra charge).

The education authority / school is not able to disclose information from a pupil's educational records if it is:

- subject to orders under the Data Protection Act 1998;
- sensitive personal data, e.g. Information about that pupil's:
  - racial or ethnic origins;
  - political opinions;
  - religious beliefs;
  - trade union membership;
  - physical or mental health or condition;
  - sex life; or
  - commission or alleged commission of a criminal offence.
- likely that disclosure would cause significant distress or harm to the pupil or anyone else; or
- a reference given in confidence to a prospective employer or educational institution.

If parents do not think that the information they receive is accurate, then they can make a request for the inaccurate information to be rectified or erased. If the education authority or school agrees that the information is inaccurate, then they must rectify or erase the inaccurate information (together with any expression of opinion which appears to be based on the inaccurate information). If they do not agree then they must tell the parent why they think the information is accurate.

If a child moves school, their educational records must be sent to the new school (free of charge) within 15 school days if the new school asks for them. Educational records have to be kept for a period of five years after a pupil has left school altogether.

Co-ordinated Support Plan

The section on **Co-ordinated support plans** provides information on what they contain and who is eligible. A CSP must be kept by the education authority at an appropriate place and must be available for inspection there (free of charge) by the parent or young person on request, during the normal hours of business of that place.

A copy of the CSP must be kept at the child or young person's school and it should be kept as part of the pupil's progress record

Transfer

Where a child or young person with a CSP moves to a different authority area, the original authority must transfer the plan to the new authority within 4 weeks of the date of moving (or 4 weeks starting on the date it becomes aware of the move) and, at the same time, provide the new authority with the names and other appropriate contact details for the agencies or people providing support in terms of the CSP.

On transfer, the CSP is treated as if it had been prepared by the new authority. The new authority must inform the parent or young person and those providing support under the CSP that the plan has been transferred and the name and other appropriate contact details for the new co-ordinator for the CSP.

Disclosure

A CSP must not be disclosed without the consent of the parent or young person, except:

* where it is necessary to do so in the interests of the child or young person;
* for the purposes of mediation, dispute resolution or appeal to the Additional Support Needs Tribunals;
* to the co-ordinator for the CSP;
* to HM Inspectorate of Schools;
* to the Scottish Ministers for the purposes of deciding whether or not to make a statutory order or direction to an education authority;
* for the purposes of educational research (but only if, the researcher undertakes not to disclose or publish anything which identifies any individual);
* on the order of any court; or
* to the Children's Reporter in connection with their statutory functions.

Discontinuance, retention and destruction

Where a CSP is to be discontinued as a result of a decision of the authority on review, the authority must not discontinue the plan before the expiry of the deadline for appealing the authority's decision to the Additional Support Needs Tribunals (i.e. 2 months).

Where a CSP is to be discontinued on review or because the authority are no longer responsible for the child or young person's school education, they must retain the CSP for 5 years and thereafter destroy it.

Where a CSP is to be discontinued because a Tribunal has ruled that the child or young person does not require a CSP, the parent or young person can elect to have the CSP retained for 5 years but, otherwise, it must be destroyed immediately.

While a CSP is being retained, the same rules on disclosure apply (as above).

Data Protection

The law gives individuals rights in respect of personal information held on computer or as part of a "relevant filing system" (including paper records). Even if information is not computerised or held in a relevant filing system, data protection rules also apply to any record of information which is processed by an education authority for educational purposes (other than information which is processed by a teacher solely for the teacher's own use).

Parents have a right to access any information held about themselves. If a child is too young to make his/her own request, a parent can make it on the child's behalf. Requests to access information must be made in writing (including email) and a fee is payable if a copy is required. The fee will vary according to the number of pages of information requested, but will not exceed £50 for educational records.

Within 40 days of a request, the "data controller" (in this case the school or education authority) must tell the parent or pupil what information it has about the pupil, why it has it and to whom it is being/has been disclosed. The parent or pupil should also receive a copy of the information and any further information needed to be able to make sense of it. For example, if the school uses abbreviations or codes, a key should be provided. The source of any information should also be made known.

The above rights do not apply where disclosure would allow another individual to be identified (this does not apply to teachers or other educational professionals), unless they have consented or it would otherwise be reasonable to disclose the information. It may be possible to anonymise the information, which will allow it to be disclosed.

If a child has legal capacity (children over 12 are presumed to have legal capacity) then educational records will not be disclosed to parents (under data protection rules) if the child objects to that disclosure. Parents may still be able to access these records under the regulations on pupils' educational records.

If the data controller is not complying with a request properly, legal action can be taken for an order to force them to comply. A complaint can be made to the Information Commissioner (UK) as well.

How can parents correct errors?

If information held about a pupil is factually inaccurate, then the parent or pupil is entitled to have it corrected. Information is inaccurate if it is incorrect or misleading in any matter of fact. Parents and pupils concerned can apply to the court for an order to correct or erase the inaccurate information. There may be an entitlement to compensation if the error has caused damage (e.g. financial or educational) to parent or pupil.

If the education authority refuses the request to amend an educational record, the parent or pupil can ask the Information Commissioner (UK) to order the correction or removal of inaccurate information.

Can people complain?

The Information Commissioner has powers to investigate complaints about the way information is being handled or about requests for access to information. If the Commissioner finds any wrongdoing, they may serve information notices, requiring the school or education authority to put things right. This may lead to further enforcement action.

See also

Additional Support for Learning
Complaints
Co-ordinated Support Plans

Useful organisations

Enquire
Independent Special Education Advice (Scotland)
Information Commissioner
Parentzone

Useful publications

Scottish Consumer Council (2001) *What's On My Record: A practical guide to your rights of access to personal information* (available from Consumer Focus Scotland)

Legal references used in this section

Reg 10 of the Schools General (Scotland) Regulations 1975

Pupils' Educational Records (Scotland) Regulations 2003, as amended

Additional Support for Learning (Co-ordinated Support Plan) (Scotland) Amendment Regulations 2005

Sections 2, 13, 14, 42; Data Protection Act 1998

Data Protection (Miscellaneous Subject Access Exemptions) Order 2000

RACE DISCRIMINATION

Race Discrimination

Race discrimination can occur in two ways:

- **Directly** – treating a person, on "racial grounds", less favourably than other people in similar circumstances;
- **Indirectly** – where a rule or condition which, on the face of it, applies to everyone actually affects one "racial group" significantly more than others, to their detriment, and this cannot be justified by other (lawful) reasons.

"Racial grounds" means on the grounds of colour, race, nationality or ethnic or national origins. "Racial group" means a group of people defined by reference to their colour, race, nationality or ethnic or national origins. People often belong to more than one racial group.

Direct discrimination can take many forms. In a school setting this might include racist insults or comments, racially motivated harassment, or more subtle differences in marking or treatment. The education authority and schools must take steps to protect children from unlawful discrimination at school. If they fail to do so, then they may be held responsible for the discriminatory actions of others (e.g. a pupil, member of staff or a visitor to the school).

Indirect discrimination can sometimes be justified by other (lawful) reasons. In schools, there would have to be educational grounds for most (if not all) cases where justification is claimed. Any potential justification must outweigh the disadvantage suffered by the person(s) affected.

For example, a school uniform rule insisting that boys wear caps was held by the courts to be indirect discrimination, because it adversely affected those who were required to wear turbans for cultural reasons. However, it would not be discrimination to ban Sikh ceremonial daggers, nor Scottish dirks, from school because this is justifiable on the grounds of safety.

It is unlawful for schools to discriminate on the grounds of race in any of the following areas:

• decisions or policies on admission;
• access to educational benefits, grants, bursaries, facilities, or other services;
• school meals, transport or uniform;
• exclusions; or
• by subjecting pupils to any other disadvantage on racial grounds.

General Duties

The education authority must not discriminate when carrying out any of its education functions and must make sure that facilities for education and any ancillary benefits are provided without race discrimination. Education authorities and grant-aided schools are subject to a race equality duty (see **Equal opportunities and equality duties** for more information).

Exclusions

It is unlawful to racially discriminate by excluding a pupil from school. Schools should take care that the same disciplinary rules are applied equally to all pupils and that these do not unfairly disadvantage one group.

There would be indirect discrimination if a school's decisions about exclusions affected proportionally more pupils from one racial group and this could not be justified on educational (or disciplinary) grounds.

Assessment

It is direct discrimination if a pupil is given lower marks on racial grounds. This can come from overt prejudice, or unconscious assumptions about the relative abilities and characteristics of different racial groups.

Indirect discrimination might occur where assessment criteria are culturally biased. For example, testing which assumes knowledge of a predominantly white European interest might be discriminatory.

Remedies

Where there has been discrimination in the delivery of education, either by the education authority or by an independent or grant-aided school, the person affected has the right to complain, and/or to raise legal action in the courts. Specialist advice should be sought from the Equality and Human Rights Commission or a solicitor.

See also

Equal opportunities and equality duties
School development plans

Useful organisations

Equalities and Human Rights Commission

Useful publications

Equalities and Human Rights Commission (undated) *A guide for further and higher education institutions in Scotland*

Equalities and Human Rights Commission (undated) *The duty to promote race equality a guide for education authorities and schools in Scotland*

Legal references used in this section

Sections 1, 3, 17, 18, 19, 71; Race Relations Act 1976

Section 2; Race Relations (Amendment) Act 2000

Race Relations Act 1976 (Statutory Duties) (Scotland) Order 2002

Mandla v. Dowell Lee [1983] 2 AC 548

RELIGION OR BELIEF: DISCRIMINATION

Religion in Scottish Schools

In Scottish education there are long-standing rules which provide a level of legal protection from discrimination on the grounds of religion.

All publicly-funded schools (including denominational schools) must be open to pupils of all denominations – this includes all religions, or those of no religion at all. Pupils must not be put at any disadvantage: due to their denomination (or their parent's denomination); nor due to a decision to withdraw from religious education or observance.

The right of boarders at publicly funded schools to attend worship and otherwise practice their (or their parents') religion outside of school times is also protected.

Discrimination on the grounds of religion or belief

Discrimination on the grounds of religion or belief is unlawful in schools. In this context, "belief" includes any religious or philosophical belief and religion or belief includes the lack of religion or belief.

Unlawful discrimination can be by way of direct discrimination or indirect discrimination. Direct discrimination is where someone is treated less favourably than someone else because of their religion or belief (or because of the religion or belief they are thought to have). Indirect discrimination is where a policy, rule or practice applies across the board but presents a particular disadvantage for one religion or belief.

Indirect discrimination is only unlawful if it cannot be reasonably justified by reference to matters other than the person's religion or belief.

Discrimination in schools

In all schools in Scotland, whether authority, independent or grant-aided schools, it is unlawful to discriminate against a pupil or prospective pupil:

1. by refusing them admission;

2. in the terms of any admission;

3. in the benefits, facilities or services offered by the school;

4. by refusing them access to any benefit, facility or service;

5. by excluding them from the school; or

6. by subjecting them to any other detriment.

Exceptions

Denominational schools in Scotland (including independent denominational schools) are only subject to the prohibition on discrimination by exclusion from school or subjecting pupils to detriment. That is, headings 1 to 4 do not apply to denominational schools.

Headings 3, 4 and 6 do not apply to anything done in connection with the content of the curriculum, or acts of worship or religious observance organised by or with the school.

Discrimination by education authorities

It is unlawful for an education authority to discriminate in the exercise of their functions.

Exceptions

The prohibition on discrimination by education authorities does not apply to the exercise of their functions relating to:

• provision, maintenance and equipment of schools;

• transport; or

• provision of travelling facilities or expenses, accommodation or board and lodging required due to a pupil's exceptional circumstances.

Where there has been discrimination in the delivery of education, either by the education authority or by an independent or grant-aided school, the person affected has the right to complain, and/or to raise legal action in the courts. Specialist advice should be sought from the Equality and Human Rights Commission or a solicitor.

Before bring legal action against a school or education authority, the person bring the action must first give written notice to the Scottish Ministers.

See also

Equal opportunities and equality duties
Human rights

Useful organisations

Equalities and Human Rights Commission
Scottish Catholic Education Service
Scottish Muslim Parents Association

Legal references used in this section

Sections 9, 10; Education (Scotland) Act 1980

Sections 49 to 51 of the Equality Act 2006

RELIGIOUS EDUCATION AND OBSERVANCE

All schools (with the possible exception of some independent schools) must be open to pupils of any religion or denomination. It has long been the custom in Scottish schools for religious observance to be practised and religious education (or instruction) to be given to pupils. The law recognises this custom and the freedom for parents to withdraw their children from these elements of schooling without being subject to any other disadvantage. The law states that education authorities are free to continue this practice.

Neither "instruction" nor "observance" are defined in legislation, but instruction probably includes all religious education lessons, whereas observance would include religious assemblies and other acts of worship.

Where religious observance is practiced, this cannot be halted or discontinued without a local referendum in favour of such a move. Guidance has been issued as to the type and content of any religious observance and instruction. Religious education should be based on Christianity, while taking account of the teaching and practices of other major religions. It should promote understanding and respect for those of differing religious beliefs.

In non-denominational schools, religious observance should be of a broadly Christian character (in denominational schools, observance will be in line with the relevant denominational tradition). Where appropriate, schools may organise special acts of religious observance for adherents of particular religions.

In primary schools, pupils should take part in religious observance at least once a week. In secondary schools, this should be at least once a month, or more frequently. Religious education in secondary schools should account for approximately 5% of the timetable for S1/S2, and approximately 80 hours over two years in S3/S4.

Parents have the right to withdraw their children from religious observance and from any education in religious subjects. This might include certain lessons from classes in other subjects as well as religious education. Parents should be told about this right, and the school handbook must include information as to the provision of religious education and observance within the school, and the arrangements made for pupils withdrawn from these activities. Pupils must not be placed at a disadvantage because of their (or their parents') denomination or religion, nor because they have been withdrawn from lessons or worship.

The parental right to withdraw children from religious elements of schooling is in line with the provisions of the Human Rights Act regarding the parent's right to have their children educated in accordance with their own religious or philosophical convictions (see **Human rights** section). However, there is a possible tension with a child's own rights to freedom of thought, conscience and religion. Scots law at present indicates that the parent's will should take precedence, but it may be possible to challenge this assumption in the courts.

Children boarding at schools under the management of an education authority must be given reasonable opportunities to practice or be instructed in their parents' religion outside of school hours. The authority do not need to incur any costs in discharging this duty. Again, there is a potential conflict of rights if the child's religious beliefs do not coincide with those of the child's parents.

See also

Equal opportunities and equality duties
Human rights
Legal action
Overview - Children's rights

Useful organisations

Scottish Catholic Education Service
Scottish Muslim Parents Association

Useful publications

Scottish Executive (2004) *The Report of the Religious Observance Review Group* (available from the Scottish Government)

Legal references used in this section

Sections 8, 9, 10; Education (Scotland) Act 1980

Articles 9, 2 (of Protocol 1); European Convention on Human Rights

Schedule I(2)(e); Education (School and Placing Information) (Scotland) Regulations 1982

SOED Circular 6/91 – "Provision of Religious Education and Religious Observance in Primary and Secondary Schools"

SAFETY AND SUPERVISION

Schools must take reasonable care of their pupils and look after their safety. Depending on the circumstances, certain precautions must be taken. These may have to be greater than would be expected for adults in the same situation.

Safety and supervision in schools

The education authority must provide supervision by at least one adult (aged 18 or over) in a playground during any break time. This applies in every education authority school which is either:

- a primary school with fifty or more pupils; or
- a special school of any size.

The education authority must also take reasonable care for the safety of pupils under their charge. This includes the supervision of pupils, where that is needed to provide the reasonable care required. The duty to take reasonable care for the safety of pupils "under their charge" includes:

- on the school bus;
- on school trips;
- at school sporting events etc.

It is unlikely to include pupils who leave school at lunchtimes (especially for older children leaving with parental permission). However, schools have a responsibility to take reasonable care that children who are too young (or otherwise unable) to look after themselves do not leave school unattended. It would not generally include pupils who arrive at school very early or leave long after the school day has ended unless pupils are attending school clubs/activities outwith normal school hours. Having said that, there have been some cases where a school has been found responsible for injuries to a pupil in the school premises prior to school starting.

Standard of supervision or care

It is commonly supposed that schools have to act *in loco parentis* and that teachers and headteachers are held to the standards of the "reasonable parent". While the courts in Scotland have used this comparison in some cases, it has also been seen as an unhelpful and unrealistic standard of care to expect in other cases. For example, where a head teacher is in charge of a school of several hundred pupils, or a class teacher is dealing with the supervision of twenty or thirty young people it is unrealistic to expect such individual care for each child.

More recent cases confirm that the school (and its teachers) have a duty to take reasonable care for the safety and health of children in their charge, and to exercise care and forethought to protect children from harm. The level of supervision of care will vary, having regard to the "age, inexperience, carelessness and high spirits" of the pupils, and the nature and degree of danger involved in any given activity. For example, more planning and greater precautions will be required for a chemistry practical than for a hand-writing exercise. Teachers are expected, while supervising pupils, to meet the standard of a teacher of ordinary skill acting with ordinary care.

The law has recognised a need to take into account the nature of some pupils, including "a tendency to meddling and mischief". However, schools are not expected to foresee "every act of stupidity" that might take place as a result. This approach recognises that pupils may often contribute to their own injuries through reckless actions, and the school cannot be held entirely to blame in those circumstances.

Safety of buildings

The education authority (or independent school) must make sure that the school buildings and equipment meet current safety requirements. Schools should have well sign-posted exit routes for evacuation of the building in the event of a fire or other emergency. The school should also carry out fire drills regularly. A fire risk assessment must be carried out in relation to potential fire risks, including appropriate fire precautions. A written fire risk assessment that records these findings is required in all but the smallest schools. The risk assessment should cover staff, pupils, parents and visitors to the school (see **School Buildings** for further information).

Occupiers' Liability

The Occupiers' Liability (Scotland) Act 1960 creates a duty on the education authority to anyone who is lawfully on the premises (including pupils). The reasonableness of the care is assessed from the point of view of the pupil, so (especially in primary or special schools) extra care is required to prevent injury from features of the school premises.

Legal action

Where the school has failed in its duty of care, the education authority (or proprietor, in the case of an independent school) would be legally responsible for any reasonably foreseeable consequences of that failure. This means that the pupil or parent could take legal action in relation to any injuries sustained as a result, even where he or she may also be partly at fault. Legal advice should be sought as soon as possible. Legal Aid may be available.

See also

Advice and assistance
Legal action
School buildings

Useful organisations

Scottish Parent Council Association

Useful publications

Scottish Executive (2003) *Fire Safety in Schools* (available from the Scottish Government)

Scottish Executive (2004) *Health and Safety on Educational Excursions: A Good Practice Guide* (available from the Scottish Government)

Legal references used in this section

Fire Precautions Act 1971

Section 19; Education (Scotland) Act 1980

School Premises (General Requirements and Standards) (Scotland) Regulations 1987 (as amended)

Schools (Safety and Supervision of Pupils) (Scotland) Regulations 1990

Fire Precautions (Workplace) Regulations 1997 (as amended)

Management of Health and Safety at Work Regulations 1999

Ahmed v. City of Glasgow Council; 2000 SLT (Sh Ct) 153

Beaumont v. Surrey C.C. 66 LGR 580

Carmarthenshire County Council v. Lewis [1955] A.C. 549

Chittock v. Woodbridge School [2002] EWCA Civ. 915

Cooper v. Manchester Corp.; The Times, Feb. 13, 1959

Hunter v. Perth and Kinross Council 2001 SCLR 856

Jacques v. Oxfordshire County Council (1967) 66 LGR 440

Johanneson v. Lothian Regional Council 1996 SLT (Sh Ct) 74

Kearn-Price v. Kent County Council [2002] EWCA Civ. 1536

Lyes v. Middlesex C.C. (1962) 61 LGR 443

McPherson v. Perth and Kinross Council, 26 Jan 2001, Court of Session (Outer House)

Nicolson v. Westmorland C.C.; The Times, Oct. 25, 1962.

Perry v. King Alfred School Society (1961) The Guardian, Oct. 28

Scott v. Lothian Regional Council 1999 RepLR 15

SCHOOL BUILDINGS

Standards for schools

School buildings, like many other public buildings, must be built according to certain standards and requirements, including health and safety.

Building standards and regulations are laid down by the government. Planning permission must also be given by the local authority before a school can be built or altered. Building standards cover things like: the resistance of building materials to fire; access and escape routes; structural stability of a building; accommodation; drainage; and supply of services (water, gas, electricity). Any extensions or improvements must also meet the latest building standards.

Health and safety requirements. Education authorities have to maintain and equip their schools in such a way as to take reasonable care for the health and safety of any occupants or visitors to the school premises. They must obey any directions from the Health and Safety Executive for this purpose. People occupying or in charge of school premises must take reasonable care to make sure that anyone entering or using the building will not suffer damage or injury which may arise because of the condition of the building. This would, for example, involve keeping pupils out of classrooms while repairs are being done. The Scottish Ministers can make rules about the use of dangerous materials or apparatus in schools.

Special regulations for school premises. Apart from the normal building and health and safety regulations, education authorities must in addition provide school premises and sites that meet other requirements.

These requirements cover:

School sites and playing fields. The minimum size of school sites and playing fields is worked out according to a legally prescribed sliding scale based on pupil numbers. For example, a secondary school with 751-1,000 pupils must cover a site of at least 2.4 hectares. Nursery schools and classes must have a garden or playing space nearby; minimum standards are also laid down for the amount of playroom accommodation there. However, the Scottish Ministers can relax or modify these requirements if they consider them unreasonable or impracticable for particular schools.

School meals accommodation. Adequate and suitable accommodation must be provided for serving school meals and for washing up, even if the meals are cooked outside the school premises.

Washrooms. A sliding scale, based on pupil numbers, lays down the number of toilets. In nursery schools and classes, for example, there must be one toilet for every 10 pupils. Except in nursery schools and classes, each toilet should be lockable and partitioned to ensure privacy. Disposal facilities for sanitary towels must be provided in schools with girls beyond primary 4 classes.

Medical rooms. Every school must have a room or other suitable place for carrying out medical inspections, except when the Scottish Ministers allow inspections to take place elsewhere. The medical room must have a toilet and a wash basin with hot and cold water. A rest room with adjacent toilet and hot and cold water supply must be provided in every secondary school.

Storage and drying accommodation. Cloakrooms or lockers must be provided for storing pupils' belongings and for hanging and drying their outdoor clothing. Every school must have sufficient storage space for books and materials, furniture, and fuel.

Outdoor areas. Playgrounds or other outdoor areas must be provided right beside the school building and be properly laid out and surfaced.

Lighting. Both natural and artificial lighting must be provided. There are technical specifications which give the minimum amount of light which must reach desk tops and other working surfaces. Light fittings must be positioned in order to prevent excessive contrast or glare in normal working conditions. There must also be protection against glare from the sky and sun.

Heating, ventilation and acoustics. Detailed specifications are laid down about room temperatures and ventilation in school buildings. For example, classrooms must be at a minimum temperature of 17°C, based on readings taken three feet from the floor, and be well enough ventilated, having regard to the use they are designed for. Classrooms and other parts of the school must be suitably insulated against noise and other disturbances.

Water supply. Proper drinking water must be supplied and there must be warm water for washing in. Warm showers must have a temperature of at least 30°C but no more than 44°C.

See also

Accessibility strategies
Books, materials and equipment
Food and drink
Safety and supervision

Useful publications

Scottish Executive (2007) *The Condition Core Fact: Building Our Future: Scotland's School Estate* (available from the Scottish Government)
Scottish Executive (2007) *School Design: Optimising the Internal Environment - Building our Future: Scotland's School Estate* (available from the Scottish Government)

Legal references used in this section

Occupiers' Liability (Scotland) Act 1960

Sections 2, 4; Health and Safety at Work Act 1974

Sections 1, 19, 19A; Education (Scotland) Act 1980 (as amended)

School Premises (General Requirements and Standards) (Scotland) Regulations 1967 (as amended)

SCHOOL CLOSURES AND CHANGES

Can education authorities close or make other changes to schools?

An education authority has a wide discretion to close or make other changes to their schools. Before making a decision, however, the authority must give parents and others a chance to give their views on the proposals. In certain cases, the education authority may need consent from the Scottish Ministers as well.

What consultation is required?

The education authority must seek the views of various groups of people before deciding whether to close a school down or to make certain other "prescribed" changes. There are various detailed rules on who must be consulted for various types of proposals. The most common and important types of changes are listed below:

Closing a school or discontinuing a stage of education

Where an education authority propose to close a school or discontinue a stage of education at a school (i.e. an entire nursery department or a whole year of primary or secondary education) the authority must consult the following groups:

- the parents of every pupil attending any school affected by the proposal;
- the parents of every child expected to attend the school to be closed in the next two years;
- the parent council of any school affected by the proposal; and
- the denominational body (if applicable).

Schools affected by the proposal include schools to which pupils would be transferred as a result of a closure of discontinuation.

Relocating a school

Where an education authority propose to move a school from one site to another, the authority must consult the following group:

- the parents of pupils attending the school to be relocated;
- the parents of every child expected to attend the school within the next two years;
- the parent council of that school; and
- the denominational body (if applicable).

Changing the catchment area for a school:

- the parents of every pupil who would be asked to move schools as a result of the catchment area to be altered;
- the parents of every primary school pupil who would be asked to change the secondary school to which the pupil will be asked to transfer in the next two year;
- the parents of every pre-school child who would be asked to change the primary school which the child would attend upon reaching school age in the next two years;
- the parent council of any school whose catchment area would be altered; and
- the denominational body (if applicable).

Changing a single sex school to a co-educational school, or changing a co-educational school to a single sex school:

- the parents of every pupil attending the school;
- the parent council of that school; and
- the denominational body (if applicable).

Revision of guidelines on the priority for placing requests if school(s) are over-subscribed:

• every person making representations to the authority;

• the parent councils of every school in the authority; and

• the denominational body or bodies concerned.

It is also possible for others to put their views to the education authority, and the authority will usually take such views into account. In particular, pupils affected by a closure or change are entitled to have their views taken into consideration, if they wish to express them. The education authority do not have to undertake a formal consultation process with pupils.

The education authority might also be expected to consult more widely as a decision might be unreasonable if they did not. For example, they may consult the wider community in which the school is located, and/or teachers and other staff employed at the school.

How should parents be consulted?

The education authority will send parents notification of the proposals, and allow 28 days for representations or comments to be received in response. The notice must also inform parents where they may find full details of the proposals. It may also give notice of any meeting to be held for parents to discuss the proposed changes. Any such meeting must be at least 14 days after the notice and at a time and place convenient to parents outside normal working hours. The notification can be posted or sent home with the child, but it must reach both or all "parents" (including guardians and anyone else with parental responsibility for the pupil). For parents of children not yet at school, notification may have to be by advertisement in a local newspaper.

An education authority must announce certain proposed changes in the press. This must be timed to give at least 28 days to respond. These changes are:

• the age or timing of transfer from primary to secondary education;

- the starting date for primary school admissions; and

- guidelines for priority of admission by placing request to a particular school.

A parent council or denominational body must receive the full details of the proposal and, again, have 28 days to respond. The parent council must be consulted as a body; the fact that most members may have been consulted anyway (as parents, staff members etc.) does not alter that obligation.

The education authority must take into account all representations they receive about a particular proposal. They must have regard to the general principle that, so far as it is compatible with suitable instruction and training and avoids unreasonable public expenditure, children are to be educated in accordance with the wishes of their parents. However, schools may be lawfully closed, even in the face of parental opposition. Failure to properly and fully take these matters into account may lead to the decision being overturned by judicial review (see **Legal action** for explanation of judicial review).

Is the education authority's decision final?

In certain cases the education authority must first get permission from the Scottish Ministers before carrying out their proposals. These cases are:

- any proposal which means a primary school pupil attending a school at least 5 miles (by the nearest available route) away from the previous school;

- any proposal which means a secondary school pupil attending a school at least 10 miles (by the nearest available route) away from the previous school;

- any proposal which means that a child at a denominational school has to attend a non-denominational school; and

- (where the denomination has objected) any proposal leading to a significant deterioration in denominational schooling compared to non-denominational schools run by the education authority.

Gaelic medium education

Although not required by law, education authorities who offer Gaelic medium education (GME) are expected to inform Bòrd na Gaidhlig and the Scottish Ministers of any plans to decrease Gaelic medium education provision and to conduct a consultation with parents in any case where they propose to close GME classes, on the same basis as they would consult on a school closure proposals.

Proposals for reform

In May 2008, the Scottish Government published a consultation paper called "Safeguarding our rural schools and improving school consultation procedures: proposals for changes to legislation". These proposals, if adopted, would lead to significant changes in the procedures for consultation in relation to all schools, with additional requirements in the case of rural schools. The proposals include a requirement on the education authority to produce an "educational benefit statement" and a specific requirement to consult with pupils and staff.

The Parentzone website should have up-to-date information regarding any changes to the law in this area.

See also

Consulting parents
Denominational schools
Legal action
Parental involvement and representation

Useful organisations

Parentzone
Scottish Government

Useful publications

Scottish Consumer Council (2008) *Improving Consultation on Rural School Closures* (available from Consumer Focus Scotland)

Scottish Executive (2004) *Education Guidance Issued Under Section 13 of the Standards in Scotland's Schools etc Act 2000 on Gaelic Education* (available from the Scottish Government)

Scottish Government (2008) *Safeguarding our rural schools and improving school consultation procedures: proposals for changes to legislation*

Legal references used in this section

Sections 22A, 22B, 135; Education (Scotland) Act 1980

Education (Publication and Consultation Etc.) (Scotland) Regulations 1981, as amended

Harvey v. Strathclyde Regional Council 1989 SLT 612

Martyn Imrie for Judicial Review of a decision of Comhairlie Nan Eilean Siar, 16 July 1999, Outer House, Court of Session

SCHOOL DEVELOPMENT PLANS

Each year the headteacher of every education authority school must prepare the school development plan. A school development plan sets the objectives and strategy for parental involvement for that school based on the education authority's annual statement of education improvement objectives.

The school development plan should say clearly how the school aims to improve its standards. It should show clearly what the school will do to improve pupils' attainments and the quality of their experiences at school. It should set out the school's objectives for parental involvement and contain a statement of the education authority's ambitions for the school. It should set down the targets it aims to reach, and review how well previous targets were met (or not). It should also say what the school's priorities for improvement are.

The development plan must be prepared only after consultation. The following people have to be consulted:

• the parent council (if any);
• teachers at the school;
• other school staff or volunteers;
• bodies representative of teachers (or other staff) at the school; and
• other parents' groups.

Pupils in attendance must also be given an opportunity to make their views known before the plan is prepared.

The school development plan must include details of how and when (and if!) the head teacher will consult with pupils and involve them in decisions about the day-to-day running of the school.

An annual report must be prepared to show what has been done to put the plan into practice within the school. School development plans must be prepared annually, but often remain the same, or with only minor revisions. Occasionally, there may be a change in circumstances which requires the plan to be prepared afresh.

Parents of pupils at the school are entitled to free access to the plan and the annual report on request (and to a free copy of their summaries).

A school development plan is not a legally binding document, more a statement of the school's aims and how it will try to get there. Having said that, school inspectors do look at the development plan as part of their inspections and if a school were consistently failing to have regard to its own development plan, that would be a legitimate ground for complaint.

See also

Complaints
Consulting children
Consulting parents
Inspections and inspector's reports

Legal references used in this section

Section 6; Standards in Scotland's Schools etc. (Scotland) Act 2000, as amended

SCHOOL RULES

The education authority have a duty to ensure that their schools develop in pupils reasonable and responsible relationships, initiative and self reliance, consideration for others, good manners and attitude to work, and habits of personal hygiene and cleanliness.

These characteristics will usually be reflected in the school's rules. Each school has its own set of rules which its pupils are expected to obey.

What if parents don't agree with the school rules?

Parents are expected to encourage compliance with the school rules. Failing to allow a child to comply with them is one of the grounds for exclusion from school. A child's failure to follow school rules may lead to further sanctions in accordance with the school rules. If it is felt that the level of non-compliance would be seriously detrimental to order and discipline in the school, then this may lead to a child's exclusion. Information about school policy on discipline and school rules must be included in the written information about the school given to parents before their child starts there. This is usually contained in a school handbook.

Unreasonable, unnecessary or unfair applications of school rules may be legitimate grounds for parental complaint, although there may not always be a legal remedy.

School rules must not have a disproportionate effect on one gender, racial group, religion, belief or sexual orientation; nor involve a substantial disadvantage for pupils with disabilities. Rules that do would be unlawful, unless justified on objective grounds.

See also

Complaints
Disability discrimination
Discipline and punishment
Exclusion from school
Parental involvement and representation
Race Discrimination
Religion or belief discrimination
Sex Discrimination
Sexual orientation discrimination

Legal references used in this section

Reg. 11; Schools General (Scotland) Regulations 1975

Schedule 1(2)(k); Education (School and Placing Information) (Scotland) Regulations 1982

Wyatt v. Wilson 1994 SLT 1135

SCHOOL STARTING AGE (including deferred entry)

Children normally start school when they are aged 4 or 5. The education authority will set a "school commencement date" for each year, usually in mid-August. This date:

• determines when children legally become of "school age" and;

• determines which children the education authority is obliged to offer school places to in a particular school year.

Education authorities may have different school commencement dates, parents should contact their local council for further information.

The year in which a child starts school will depend on their age at the 'school commencement date'.

If the child is 5 years old at the school commencement date:

They are legally of school age and their parents are under an obligation to provide them with an education. This applies whether parents intend sending their child to an education authority school or educating their child in some other way.

If the child will be 5 before the 'appropriate latest date':

The education authority must make a place available at a school. The "appropriate latest date" is another date set by the education authority which is the latest date in the year when a child can have their 5th birthday to be able to enter school that year. There cannot be a gap of more than 6 months and 7 days between the appropriate latest date for one school year and the school commencement date for the following school year (mid to late February). A parent whose child's 5th birthday falls between the school commencement date and the latest appropriate date has the option to either send the child to school while they are still 4, or to defer entry until the following session when they have turned 5. However, a child may not be entitled to free nursery (or pre-school) education during this deferral year.

If the child will be 5 after the 'appropriate latest date':

If a child turns 5 between the 'appropriate latest date' for one school year and the school commencement date for the next school year, they must normally wait until the following school year to start school. For example, if a child turns 5 in mid-April 2009, they will have to wait until the school commencement date in the Autumn of 2009 to start their school education.

Can children start school early?

If a child will not turn 5 until after the 'appropriate latest date' the parent/s can ask the education authority for a place in a primary school anyway. If the education authority agreed, the child would take up their place at the start of the school term, in the example given above, the child would start school in Autumn 2008, instead of Autumn 2009. This would lead to the child beginning primary school a year earlier than would normally be the case. The education authority must agree to early entry unless the education normally provided at the school was not suited to the ability and aptitude of that child.

There is no right of appeal against a refusal of a request for an early placement. In some cases, a legal challenge may be possible by way of judicial review. (see **Legal action**)

See also

Admission to school
Legal action
Pre-school education

Useful organisations

Parentzone

Useful publications

Scottish Executive (2003) *National Care Standards – Early Education and Childcare up to the age of 16* (2003) (available from the Scottish Government)

Scottish Government (2008) *Final report from the workforce task group for the early years framework*

Legal references used in this section

Sections 31, 32; Education (Scotland) Act 1980

Section 38; Standards in Scotland's Schools etc. Act 2000

SCOTLAND'S COMMISSIONER FOR CHILDREN AND YOUNG PEOPLE

The Commissioner for Children and Young People (Scotland) Act 2003 was passed in May 2003, with the first Commissioner, Kathleen Marshall taking up the post in early 2004. The role of Scotland's Commissioner for Children and Young People is focused on the promotion and safeguarding of children's rights.

The Commissioner:

• is independent from the Scottish Government;

• has a formal status in law and statutory powers and duties;

• must use the views of children and young people themselves in the Commission's work; and

• has powers to conduct investigations (including powers to require the production of documents and attendance of witnesses).

The Commissioner's work covers all children in Scotland, up to the age of 18. In addition, the Commissioner's work covers young people under the age of 21 who have been "looked after" by a local authority (see **Looked after children**).

What does the Commissioner do?

The Commissioner's primary function is to promote and safeguard the rights of children and young people. The Commissioner is to:

• promote awareness and understanding of the rights of children and young people;

• keep under review the law, policy and practice relating to the rights of children and young people with a view to assessing its adequacy and effectiveness;

* promote best practice by service providers;
* promote, commission, undertake and publish research on matters relating to the rights of children and young people.

The Commissioner must have regard to any relevant provisions of the United Nations Convention on the Rights of the Child (see **Overview - Children's rights**) and equal opportunities requirements (see **Equal opportunities and equality duties**).

The Commissioner must promote the involvement of children and young people, and ensure this is part of the Commissioner's work. For example, the Commissioner must ensure that:

* children and young people are made aware of what the commissioner's functions, the ways they can communicate with the commissioner and the ways the commissioner can respond;
* children and young people are consulted on the work of the commissioner;
* particular attention is paid to involving children and young people who do not have other adequate means to make their views known; and
* organisations that work with and for children and young people are consulted in the work of the commissioner.

The Commissioner must prepare and keep under review a strategy for involving children and young people in their work.

The Commissioner must make an annual report to Parliament and must report on formal investigations. The Commissioner may report on any other matter. These reports must be published and there must be child-friendly versions of such reports.

The Commissioner has the power to carry out formal investigations.

What can the Commissioner investigate?

The Commissioner may carry out an investigation on the extent to which "service providers" have regard to the rights, interests and views of children and young people. This could include education providers, whether in the statutory or independent sectors.

The Commissioner may carry out such an investigation only if:

- the matter to be investigated raises an issue of particular significance to children and young people generally or to particular groups of children and young people; and
- the investigation would not duplicate work of another person.

In addition, there are limitations on what the Commissioner can investigate. She cannot investigate:

- issues which are reserved to the UK parliament;
- issues relating only to a particular child or young person;
- the making of decisions or taking of action in particular legal proceedings before a court or tribunal;
- a matter which is the subject of legal proceedings before a court or tribunal.

Scotland's Commissioner for Children and Young People is therefore not able to assist in individual cases. The correct procedures in these cases are outlined in **Appeals** and **Complaints**.

See Also

Appeals
Complaints
Human Rights
Overview - Children's Rights

Useful organisations

Article 12
Children in Scotland
Scotland's Commissioner for Children and Young People

Legal references used

Commissioner for Children and Young People (Scotland) Act 2003

THE SCOTTISH PARLIAMENT AND SCOTTISH GOVERNMENT

The Scottish Parliament

Following the referendum on devolution in 1997, the Scotland Act 1998 established the Scottish Parliament. The first elections to the Scottish Parliament took place in 1999 and elections must take place every 4 years.

The Scottish Parliament has the power to make new laws for Scotland. However, there are restrictions on its "legislative competence" (i.e. the laws it is allowed to make):

• it is not allowed to legislate on "reserved matters", which are reserved to Westminster. These include consumer protection, defence, employment, equal opportunities, and social security, among some other policy areas. Education is not a reserved matter and so the Scottish Parliament can make laws relating to Education.

• it can only make laws which are compatible with the European Convention on Human Rights (see **Human rights** section)

If the Scottish Parliament made a law that was outwith its legislative competence, it would not be a law at all. If a court is considering a case, and the issue of whether an Act of the Scottish Parliament is within its legislative competence, this is called a "devolution issue." The Advocate General and the Lord Advocate must be told about any devolution issues and be given the opportunity to become involved in the case. Lower courts can refer devolution issues to the Inner House of the Court of Session or the High Court for a decision.

The Scottish Government is led by the First Minister and the Ministers appointed by him or her. The Scottish Ministers have administrative back up from civil servants who work in the Scottish Government. The Scottish Government is organised into five core strategic objectives, which are further split into over fifty directorates. The Scottish Government's Schools Directorate is responsible for administering government policy in relation to school education.

The Scottish Government issues guidance and circulars on education matters and funds research into related issues. It funds various non-departmental public bodies, such as the Scottish Children's Reporter Administration.

Useful organisations

Scottish Government
Scottish Parliament

SECURE RESIDENTIAL SCHOOLS

A secure residential school is a school with boarding accommodation where children who are experiencing difficulties may be required to stay. Most children who attend residential schools do so under the authority of a children's hearing (see **Children's hearing** section for more information). A small number of children will be there because of an order from the Sheriff or High Court, or by voluntary arrangement with their parents. Generally speaking, children who are placed in secure residential schools will have a level of social work involvement.

Many admissions to residential school will be on a planned basis, with children and their parents having the opportunity to visit the school, meet staff and residents and talk over any questions they may have.

Teaching

Secure residential schools usually offer much smaller classes than mainstream schools, and tend to have a more limited range of subjects. There is usually provision for children to sit standard grade exams or obtain vocational qualifications. They are staffed by both teachers and care or residential staff, who are able to offer the young people additional support.

Contact with children

If a child is placed in a secure residential school, the local authority has an obligation to maintain and encourage contact between the child and their family. Contact arrangements should normally be discussed before a child is placed in a secure residential school. If a children's hearing authorises the child's placement in a residential school, then before coming to their decision, they must also consider what contact arrangements are necessary. Most children in residential schools will have some level of home leave, although the withdrawal of home leave may be used as a sanction for misbehaviour.

Corporal punishment

Corporal punishment is not allowed in residential schools, although staff in residential schools are trained in restraint techniques which are used if residents are behaving in a way which poses a risk to themselves or others.

Additional support needs

Children who require to be educated in secure residential schools will, in most instances, satisfy the legal tests and be assessed as having additional support needs (see **Additional Support for Learning**). If they receive significant levels of social work support which is provided at school or related to their school education, they may well satisfy the criteria for a Co-ordinated Support Plan as well (see **Co-ordinated Support Plans**). If so, the authority will have additional duties to make provision for their needs.

See also

Additional Support for Learning
Looked after children
Children's hearings
Co-ordinated Support Plans
Inspections and inspection reports
Physical intervention and restraint

Useful organisations

Enquire
HM Inspectorate of Education
Independent Special Education Advice (Scotland)
Scottish Government

Useful publications

British Institute of Learning Disability (2004) *Easy Guide to Being Held Safely* (available from the British Institute of Learning Disability)

Asquith, Stewart (Ed) (1995) *The Kilbrandon Report: Children And Young Persons Scotland* (available on the Children's Hearings website www.childrens-hearings.co.uk)

Legal references used in this section

Part 2; Children (Scotland) Act 1995

SEX DISCRIMINATION

Sex discrimination can occur in two ways:

• **Directly** – treating a person, on the grounds of the person's sex, less favourably than someone of the opposite sex in similar circumstances;

• **Indirectly** – where a rule or condition which, on its face, applies to everyone, actually affects one sex a lot more than the other, to a person's detriment, and this cannot be justified by other (lawful) reasons.

The laws on sex discrimination now protect against discrimination on the grounds of gender, marital status and transgender status (gender reassignment).

Direct discrimination can take many forms. In a school setting this might include sexist insults or comments, sexual harassment, or subtle differences in marking or treatment. The education authority and the school must take reasonable steps to protect children from unlawful sex discrimination at school. If they do not, then the education authority may be held responsible for the discriminatory actions of pupils, staff or even visitors to the school.

Indirect discrimination can sometimes be justified by other (lawful) reasons. In schools, there should normally be an educational justification for differences of this type. Any potential justification must outweigh the disadvantage suffered by the person affected.

It is unlawful for schools to discriminate on the grounds of a person's sex in any of the following:

- decisions or policies on admission;
- access to educational benefits, grants, bursaries, facilities, or other services;
- school meals, transport or uniform;
- exclusions; or
- by subjecting pupils to any other detriment or disadvantage.

In general, the education authority must not discriminate when carrying out any of their education functions and must make sure that facilities for education and any ancillary benefits are provided without sex discrimination. It must also comply with its gender equality duty (see Equal opportunities and equality duties).

Admissions

Schools which normally admit both boys and girls would be breaking the law if they refused to admit pupils on the grounds of their sex or made it more difficult for one sex. However, this does not apply to single sex schools or schools which are primarily single sex.

Accommodation

Schools with boarding accommodation for boys and girls are not allowed to refuse accommodation on the grounds of sex. Schools with accommodation for only one sex may do so, even if they educate both sexes. Accommodation at mixed residences can be refused, however, if this would mean a pupil having to share sleeping, washing or other facilities with the opposite sex.

Exclusions

It is unlawful to discriminate of grounds of sex by excluding a pupil from school. Schools should make sure the same rules are applied to all pupils and that these do not unfairly disadvantage one gender.

Many more boys than girls are excluded in mixed gender schools. However this would only count as indirect sex discrimination if it is because girls are being showed some sort of unfair preference, or there were different behavioural expectations for boys than girls.

There would be indirect discrimination if a school's policy on exclusions affected proportionally more boys than girls (or vice-versa) and this could not be justified on educational grounds.

Assessment

It is direct discrimination if a child is given lower marks because of his or her sex. This can come from overt prejudice, or unconscious assumptions about the relative abilities and characteristics of male and female pupils.

It might be indirect discrimination if assessment criteria are gender biased: for example testing which assumes knowledge of predominantly male interests might be discriminatory.

Dress and Uniform

Certain differences in uniform on the grounds of sex have been held to be lawful, as long as similar (though not necessarily identical) restrictions apply to the opposite sex. For example, it would not be unlawful sex discrimination to insist that boys wear ties if the uniform code for girls is similarly smart.

Remedies

Where there has been sex discrimination in the delivery of education, either by the education authority or by an independent or grant-aided school, the pupil affected has the right to complain, and/or to raise legal action in the courts. Specialist advice is available from the Equality and Human Rights Commission or a solicitor.

See also

Clothing and uniform
Equal opportunities and equality duties
Human rights
Legal action

Useful organisations

Equalities and Human Rights Commission

Useful publications

Equal Opportunities Commission (undated) *An Equal Opportunities Guide for Parents* (available from the Equalities and Human Rights Commission)

Legal references used in this section

Sections 1, 2, 22, 23, 25, 26, 46, 66; Sex Discrimination Act 1975

SEX EDUCATION

Sex education is seen as an integral part of a child's personal, social and health education. The Scottish Government has issued guidance to education authorities on the manner in which sex education should be conducted, and education authorities must have regard to this. The guidance outlines the purpose of sex education as being "to provide knowledge and understanding of the nature of sexuality and the processes of human reproduction within the context of relationships based on love and respect." There is to be an emphasis on the importance of commitment, and respect in relationships, and on the responsibilities of both partners in a sexual relationship.

Education authorities also have a general duty, when performing their functions, in relation to school–age children to have regard to:

• the value of stable family life in a child's development; and
• the need to ensure that the content of instruction provided in the performance of those functions is appropriate, having regard to each child's age, understanding and stage of development.

Scottish Government Guidance states that schools should consult parents and carers when developing their sex education programmes. Parents and carers should have the opportunity to examine the materials which will be used, in advance.

Where parents have concerns about what their children will be taught, they can make an appointment with the head teacher, who will explain the purpose of sex education, and will go over what children will be taught. If parents are still unhappy with their children attending these classes, they can withdraw the child from them. If so, the child should be given an alternative class to attend while his or her classmates are receiving sex education. Matters relating to sex, sexuality and morality may come up in other classes within the curriculum. It is not possible to have a child withdrawn from classes where these matters *may* arise.

If there are concerns about the information or materials a child has been given, parents should take this up with the head teacher in the first instance. If dissatisfied with the response, they are also able to take the matter up with the education authority directly.

See also

Complaints
Curriculum (what is taught)

Useful organisations

Learning and Teaching Scotland
Parentzone

Useful publications

Learning and Teaching Scotland (2000) *Health Education 5 – 14 National Guidelines*

Learning and Teaching Scotland (2000) *Sex Education in Scottish Schools: a guide for parents and carers*

Scottish Executive (2000) *Report of the Working Group on Sex Education in Scottish Secondary Schools* (available from the Scottish Government)

Legal references used in this section

Standards in Scotland's Schools etc. (Scotland) Act 2000, Section 56

Scottish Executive Circular 2/2001 "Standards in Scotland's Schools etc. Act 2000: Conduct of Sex Education in Scottish Schools"

Section 35; Ethical Standards in Public Life etc. (Scotland) Act 2000

SEXUAL ORIENTATION: DISCRIMINATION

Discrimination on the grounds of sexual orientation

Discrimination on the grounds of sexual orientation is unlawful in schools. Unlawful discrimination can be by way of direct discrimination or indirect discrimination. Direct discrimination is where someone is treated less favourably than someone else because of their sexual orientation (or because of the sexual orientation they are thought to have). Indirect discrimination is where a policy, rule or practice applies across the board but presents a particular disadvantage for people of a particular sexual orientation.

Indirect discrimination is only unlawful if it cannot be reasonably justified by reference to matters other than the person's sexual orientation.

In all schools in Scotland, whether authority, independent or grant-aided schools, it is unlawful to discriminate against a pupil or prospective pupil:

- by refusing them admission;
- in the terms of any admission;
- in the benefits, facilities or services offered by the school;
- by refusing them access to any benefit, facility or service;
- by excluding them from the school; or
- by subjecting them to any other detriment.

It is also unlawful for an education authority to discriminate in the exercise of their functions.

Remedies

Where there has been discrimination in the delivery of education, either by the education authority or by an independent or grant-aided school, the person affected has the right to complain, and/or to raise legal action in the courts. Specialist advice should be sought from the Equality and Human Rights Commission or a solicitor.

Before bring legal action against a school or education authority, the person bring the action must first give written notice to the Scottish Ministers.

See also

Equal opportunities and equalities duties
Human rights
Legal action

Useful organisations

Childline
Equalities and Human Rights Commission
LGBT Youth Scotland
Parentline
Parentzone

Legal references used in this section

Equality Act (Sexual Orientation) Regulations 2007

SPECIAL ABILITIES AND APTITUDES

Some children may have special talents or aptitudes, either generally or in specific subjects, which may require additional support to reach their fullest potential.

The education authority must provide parents, on request, with information about their policies and practices for educating children with special talents. The Scottish Executive made funds available to set up and support schools with specialist facilities which cater for children with special talents in particular subjects, such as sport, music, traditional music, dance and international languages. Study may be available by way of distance learning, or in the evening and at weekends. Intake to such schools is limited and is based on aptitude in the chosen subject.

The education authority has a general duty to provide an adequate and efficient education and in providing that education, must have regard to each child's aptitudes and abilities. School education must also be directed to developing a child's personality, talents and mental and physical abilities to the child's fullest potential.

Able pupils may be assessed as having additional support needs if they require educational provision in addition to (or different from) that provided in schools to children of the same age. If so, the education authority have specific duties to make provision for those needs. (see **Additional Support for Learning**)

Where able pupils also require significant additional support from another "appropriate agency" e.g. a further or higher education institution, they may require a Co-ordinated Support

Plan. If so, the authority has additional duties to the child or young person in question (see **Co-ordinated Support Plans**).

See also

Additional Support for Learning
Complaints
Co-ordinated Support Plans
Legal action

Useful organisations

Enquire
Independent Special Education Advice (Scotland)

Useful publications

Smith, C. (2005) *Teaching Gifted and Talented Pupils in the Primary School: A Practical Guide* (available from Scottish Network for Able Pupils)

Sutherland, M. (2005) *Gifted and Talented in the Early Years: Practical Activities for Children aged 3 to 5* (available from Scottish Network for Able Pupils)

Legal references used in this section

Schedule I,(3)(o) of the Education (Schools and Placing Information) (Scotland) Regulations 1982

Section 1 of the Education (Scotland) Act 1980

Section 2(1) of the Standards in Scotland's Schools etc. (Scotland) Act 2000

Sections 1, 2 & 4 of the Education (Additional Support for Learning) (Scotland) Act 2004

RB v. The Highland Council 2007 FamLR 115

STANDARDS IN SCHOOL EDUCATION

At a national level

There is an obligation on the Scottish Ministers to try to improve the quality of education in Scotland. When making decisions about educational provision, they must have regard to this duty. They must also set National Priorities in Education after consultation with education authorities and other bodies.

The National Priorities in Education are currently::

1. To raise standards of educational attainment for all in schools, especially in the core skills of literacy and numeracy, and to achieve better levels in national measures of achievement including examination results;

2. To support and develop the skills of teachers, the self-discipline of pupils and to enhance school environments so that they are conducive to teaching and learning;

3. To promote equality and help every pupil benefit from education, with particular regard paid to pupils with disabilities and additional support needs, and to Gaelic and other lesser used languages;

4. To work with parents to teach pupils respect for self and one another and their interdependence with other members of their neighbourhood and society and to teach them the duties and responsibilities of citizenship in a democratic society; and

5. To equip pupils with the foundation skills, attitudes and expectations necessary to prosper in a changing society and to encourage creativity and ambition.

At education authority level

Education authorities, too, have a duty to try to improve the quality of school education in their area, and must make an "annual statement of education improvement objectives". This must include a description of:

- how the authority will involve parents in promoting the education of their children (prepared as part of the authority's strategy for parental involvement);
- how it encourages equal opportunities;
- the circumstances in which it will provide gaelic medium education;

The annual statement will also set objectives relating to the national priorities in education (and other matters as the education authority sees fit).

Each education authority must then publish an annual report on how well it has achieved the objectives it has set itself.

At individual school level

Schools too have responsibilities in improving the standards in education. Head teachers, on behalf of the education authority, must prepare a "school development plan" for their school, setting out the objectives for that school in implementing the education authority's own annual statement of education improvement objectives. Teachers, pupils, parents and others are consulted about what should be in the school development plan. Then an annual report is published on what was done to implement the plan. Copies of the development plan and the annual report should be made available free of charge to parents.

Review of school performance

Education authorities define and publish standards of performance for measuring the quality of education in schools managed by them. The authority must then review the quality of education provided at each school against the measures and standards set by them. "Quality of education" includes the extent of parental involvement in their child's education.

Having reviewed a school, if the authority concludes that it is not performing satisfactorily, they must take the necessary steps to remedy the problem.

See also

Consulting with children
Consulting with parents
Inspection and inspector's reports
School development plans

Useful organisations

HM Inspectorate of Education
Scottish Government
Parentzone

Useful publications

Scottish Government (current edition) *Attendance and Absence in Scottish Schools*

Scottish Government (current edition) *Destinations of Leavers from Scottish Secondary Schools*

Scottish Government (current edition) *Examination Results in Scottish Schools*

Scottish Government (current edition) *Scottish Schools: costs*

Legal references used in this section

Sections 4, 5, 6, 7; Standards in Scotland's Schools etc. Act 2000, as amended

The Education (National Priorities) (Scotland) Order 2000

TEACHERS' CONDITIONS OF SERVICE

Teachers' terms of employment

The conditions under which teachers are employed are mainly governed by national-level negotiation between the teaching profession and local authorities. The Scottish Negotiating Committee for Teachers (SNCT) is made up of representatives of the teaching unions, local authorities and the Scottish Government. They cover matters like: teachers' working hours; how much class teaching is done; grievance and discipline procedures; absences and other matters. Some other matters will be decided locally, and you can find details of local agreements on the SNCT website.

These arrangements do not apply to teachers in independent schools.

Teachers are also bound by the terms of the contract of employment with their employers. This includes the express written terms and certain other duties implied at common law into contracts of employment. For example there is a general duty on teachers to obey all reasonable instructions given by their employers.

Teachers' qualifications

These are the qualifications which teachers must normally have if trained in Scotland:

• Primary teachers must hold either a degree in primary education or a Post Graduate Certificate in Education;

• Secondary teachers must hold a university degree in a relevant subject and a Post Graduate Certificate in Education, or a degree in their chosen subject which includes a teaching qualification.

Under European Law, teachers with equivalent teaching qualifications from other EU countries must be allowed to teach in UK schools.

Once qualified, in order to teach in a local authority school or Jordanhill School, all teachers must register with the General Teaching Council for Scotland. Registration is not legally required for teaching in independent schools, although in practice most independent schools do insist on registration. Teachers are registered provisionally at first, until they complete a probationary period of one year satisfactorily. At any stage in a teacher's career, registration can be withdrawn as a result of criminal conviction or professional misconduct.

Qualifications for teaching hearing impaired or visually impaired pupils

Where an education authority employ a teacher wholly or mainly to teach hearing impaired pupils that teacher must have, or be in the process of obtaining, an appropriate qualification to teach such pupils.

Where an education authority employ a teacher wholly or mainly to teach visually impaired pupils that teacher must have, or be in the process of obtaining, an appropriate qualification to teach such pupils.

Where an education authority employ a teacher wholly or mainly to teach pupils who are both hearing and visually impaired that teacher must have, or be in the process of obtaining, an appropriate qualification to teach such pupils.

Working hours

The working year for teachers is 195 days. 190 days coincide with the school year for pupils and the remaining five days are worked by the individual teachers on duties as planned by the council (often as in-service training).

A teacher's working week is 35 hours, excluding lunch and breaks. Class contact time is set at a maximum of 22.5 hours per week (15.75 hours per week for probationer teachers). Teachers are entitled to a weekly allowance of time not less than one-third of class contact time, for preparation and marking. The use of remaining time will be subject to agreement at school level within guidelines. Any tasks which do not require a teacher's physical presence at the school can be carried out at a time and place of his or her choosing.

Teachers do not have to take part in activities outside of school time, such as school clubs or sports fixtures.

Industrial action

Teachers have the same rights as other employees in an industrial dispute, and are very unlikely to be dismissed for participating in an official strike. During industrial action, the education authority has a legal obligation to take whatever reasonable steps are necessary to ensure that services are kept running where possible. Where an education authority is not taking adequate steps to ensure children's access to education during an industrial dispute, parents may complain to the Scottish Ministers or take legal action. The Scottish Ministers or the court would then have to decide whether, in view of the industrial action, the education authority had nonetheless acted reasonably in fulfilling or attempting to fulfil their duties to provide children with school education.

Where possible, the school should inform parents of industrial action before it takes place so that they can make alternative arrangements for their childcare etc.

See also

Complaints
Legal action

Useful organisations

General Teaching Council for Scotland
Learning and Teaching Scotland
Parentzone

Useful publications

Scottish Executive (2001) *A Teaching Profession for the 21st Century: Agreement reached following recommendations made in the McCrone Report* (available from the Scottish Government)

Legal references used in this section

European Communities (Recognition of Professional Qualifications) Regulations 1991

Requirements for Teachers (Scotland) Regulations 2005

Section 70 of the Education (Scotland) Act 1980

Walker v. Strathclyde Regional Council 1986 SLT 523.

TRANSPORT

The education authority must, when necessary, arrange transport for pupils to get to school and back. Transport may be provided by the education authority's own buses or contracted transport. Taxis and private cars are often used. In more remote areas, ferries and even aircraft are sometimes used. The law specifically mentions providing bicycles for pupils to use, but there are not thought to be many examples of this in practice. The authority has the option to pay all or some of the travelling expenses for a child to attend school instead of directly providing transport or contracting it to someone else.

Written information about transport arrangements must be provided to parents, including entitlement to free school transport where available.

Free school transport

Free school transport must be provided for children who live further than the "statutory walking distance" away from the school. This is:

• for pupils under 8 years old, two miles; and
• for pupils aged 8 or more, three miles.

This entitlement to free school transport does not apply if a child attends a school other than the local school (or other school nominated by the education authority in accordance with its published arrangements for placing children in schools) because the child's parent made a placing request. In that case, parents will usually have to make their own arrangements for travel. Neither does it apply to nursery or pre-school education (unless the child has a Co-ordinated Support Plan), although the education authority may always provide assistance or transport if it wishes (see

Co-ordinated Support Plans). The education authority, in deciding whether or not to provide school transport, must act lawfully and reasonably. A failure to do so could lead to legal action.

Free school transport does not have to be provided for the whole distance, so long as the distance a child needs to walk is less than the statutory walking distance. So, for example, there may be a walk from the house to the bus stop and a walk from the bus stop to the school, which can be anything up to 2 or 3 miles (depending on the child's age).

In remote areas, the education authority may offer boarding accommodation in hostels provided and maintained for pupils rather than transport.

Lack of suitable transport is listed as a potential reasonable excuse for non-attendance at school. This may apply where the route, though shorter than the statutory walking distance, is hazardous or otherwise unsuitable for children. In these circumstances, the education authority still has an obligation to provide education for a child. The simplest way of meeting this obligation is by providing free transport.

The education authority has discretion to offer free transport to any pupil. In deciding whether or not to do so, it must consider (among other things) the safety of the pupil concerned. It must offer spare places on a school bus (or other vehicle used for school transport) to pupils who would not otherwise be entitled to free school transport. The authority has discretion to charge for these places. These "courtesy places" may have to be given up if the number of pupils entitled to free transport increases. The education authority should give adequate notice to allow alternative arrangements to be made if this happens. There may also have to be a period of consultation, if a change is to be made to a long-standing arrangement.

Safety on school transport

The education authority is responsible for the safety and (where appropriate) supervision of pupils on transport it provides as above. This is the case even where the vehicle itself is provided by a private company, although that company may share some of the responsibility.

Local authorities will be able to provide information relevant to local areas, through either the education department or the transport department. Each education authority should have a policy on transport to school, which will set out the steps which can be taken if the parent or young person is unhappy with the authority's decision on transport to school.

See also

Additional Support for Learning
Consulting parents

Useful organisations

Parentzone
Scottish Parent Council Association

Useful publications

Scottish School Board Association (1998) *Safe School Travel* (available from the Scottish Parent Council Association

Scottish Consumer Council (2005) *Travelling to School* (available from Consumer Focus Scotland)

Legal references used in this section

Schedule I(2)(l); Education (Schools and Placing Information) (Scotland) Regulations 1982

Sections 13, 42, 50, 51; Education (Scotland) Act 1980

Section 37; Standards in Scotland's Schools etc. Act 2000

Schools (Safety and Supervision of Pupils) (Scotland) Regulations 1990

Jacques v. Oxfordshire County Council (1967) 66 LGR 440

GG v. Glasgow City Council, unreported, Court of Session (Outer House) 11 July 2001

TRAVELLERS AND GYPSIES/TRAVELLERS

The education authority's duty towards children in their area

An education authority has a duty to provide education to all the children in their area, regardless of whether the children are nationals of the UK, EC or some other state. Similarly, the parents of such children are under an obligation to ensure their children are educated (whether at school or otherwise).

Children of mobile workers

If parents work away from home a lot, the education authority can either provide boarding accommodation for children while parents are away or arrange for the education authority in the area where parents are staying to provide education on the "home" education authority's behalf. Education authorities are under no obligation to do so. They will take into account what other provisions parents could make for their children's care and what would be in the children's educational interests.

Travelling children

If Gypsies/Travellers feel that the education authority's policy towards school education for their children is discriminatory, they may be able to challenge the policy on the basis of the Race Relations Act 1976. The Scottish Government's position is that all policies should be framed on the understanding that Gypsies/Travellers have distinct ethnic characteristics and should therefore be regarded as an ethnic group, until such time as a court decision is made on recognition as a racial group under the Race Relations Act 1976.

On that basis, the education authority may also have duties to the Gypsies/Travellers children in terms of the Race Relations (Amendment) Act 2000.

If an itinerant lifestyle means that a child or young person requires additional support to help them reach their educational potential, then they are entitled to extra help from the education authority as having additional support needs.

The rules on attendance and authorised absences from school for the children of Travellers are complex and are not always applied in the same way. Parents should consult the Scottish Traveller Education Programme (see below) for more detailed information.

Children from other European Union (EU) member states

Children from other EU member states and their parents can expect the same education rights as their British counterparts. In addition, they are entitled to some English language tuition, and help with adapting to their new country. There is also a duty to promote teaching in the child's mother tongue, and instruction in the child's culture of origin.

Children moving out of the area

Pupils moving to another education authority area in Scotland will have the same rights in relation to education as in the previous area (although the way education authorities interpret and implement their duties may differ). The law relating to education in England, Wales and Northern Ireland is significantly different to Scots law. However, pupils moving to any of these countries, will have the same rights as other children living in the new area.

Pupils moving abroad, but within the EU, will have the same rights as the nationals of the member state they move to, with additional rights for the child to receive tuition in one of the official languages of that particular country.

Where pupils are moving abroad, and outwith the EU, their rights will depend very much on the domestic law of the country moved to. Parents should check the position with the country's Embassy or High Commission.

See also

Additional Support for Learning
English as an Additional Language
Equal opportunities and equality duties
Race discrimination

Useful organisations

Enquire
Equalities and Human Rights Commission
Independent Special Education Advice (Scotland)

Useful publications

Scottish Refugee Council and Save the Children (2000) *I didn't come here for fun: listening to the views of children and young people who are refugees or asylum-seekers in Scotland*

Learning and Teaching Scotland (2003) *Inclusive Educational Approaches for Gypsies and Travellers (2003)*

Legal references used in this section

School Attendance and Absence Circular 5/03 – Addendum

USEFUL ORGANISATIONS

**Additional Support Needs Tribunals
(www.asntscotland.gov.uk)**

The Additional Support Needs Tribunals for Scotland hears appeals, called "references", from parents and young people on certain matters relating to co-ordinated support plans. The Tribunals' exercise of their statutory functions, decisions and dealings with its users and the public is independent of the Scottish Government and local authorities.

Tribunal Secretary
Office of the President of the Additional Support Needs
Tribunals for Scotland
450 Argyle Street
Glasgow G2 8LG

Tel: 0845 120 2906

Email: inquiries@asntscotland.gov.uk

Article 12 (www.article12.org)

Article 12 in Scotland is a young person led network of individuals and organisations that works across Scotland and internationally to promote young people's rights as set out in the United Nations Convention on the Rights of the Child, the European White Paper on Youth and other international human rights charters relevant to young people.

PO Box 7182
Montrose DD10 9WW

ASDAN (www.asdan.org.uk)

ASDAN creates the opportunity for learners to achieve personal and social development through the achievement of its Awards and Qualifications. These aim to recognise and reward personal skills as they are developed through activity-based 'Challenges' in such areas as sports, healthy living, community involvement, work experience, expressive arts, relationships, citizenship, personal finance and enterprise. ASDAN programmes enhance self-esteem, aspirations and individual contribution to local, national and global communities and can be achieved in a variety of educational, training, employment, youth and community situations.

Wainbrook House
Hudds Vale Road
St. George
Bristol BS5 7HY

Tel: (0117) 9411126

Email: info@asdan.org.uk

Bòrd na Gàidhlig (www.bord-na-gaidhlig.org.uk)

Bòrd na Gàidhlig was established by the Gaelic Language (Scotland) Act 2005 which aims to promote the use of Scottish Gaelic, secure the status of the language and ensure its long-term future.

Bòrd na Gàidhlig
Darach
Fèith nan Clach
Inbhir
Nis IV2 7PA

Tel: 01463 225454

Email: fios@bord-na-gaidhlig.org.uk

Capability Scotland (www.capability-scotland.org.uk)

Capability Scotland is the country's leading disability organisation working for a just Scotland. We work with disabled children and adults and their families and carers to support them in their everyday lives. We provide a diverse range of services.

11 Ellersly Road
Edinburgh EH12 6HY

Tel: 0131 313 5510

Textphone: 0131 346 2529

Care Commission (Scottish Commission for the Regulation of Care) (www.carecommission.com)

The Care Commission was set up in April 2002 under the Regulation of Care (Scotland) Act 2001 to regulate all adult, child and independent healthcare services in Scotland. They make sure that care service providers meet the Scottish Governments National Care Standards and work to improve the quality of care.

Compass House
11 Riverside Drive
Dundee DD1 4NY

Tel: 0845 603 0890

Email: enquiries@carecommission.com

Careers Scotland (www.careers-scotland.org.uk)

Provides services, information and support to: individuals at all ages and stages of career planning.

9 – 11 Renfield Street
Glasgow G2 5EZ

Tel: 0845 8 502 502

Childline (www.childline.org.uk)

ChildLine is the free 24-hour helpline for children and young people in distress or danger. Trained volunteer counsellors comfort, advise and protect children and young people who may feel they have nowhere else to turn.

As well as the main ChildLine service, ChildLine in Scotland also runs two dedicated phone lines for children and young people who are affected by particular issues: there is a dedicated freephone bullying helpline, funded by the Scottish Government and The Line, for people living away from home, for example in care at boarding school or have to spend a long time in hospital.

Helpline: 0800 1111

Bullying Line: 0800 44 11 11

The Line: 0800 88 44 44

Children in Scotland (www.childreninscotland.org.uk)

Children in Scotland is the national agency for voluntary, statutory and professional organisations and individuals working with children and their families in Scotland. Children in Scotland produces a monthly magazine for its members and subscribers and is UK publisher for Children in Europe magazine.

Princes House
5 Shandwick Place
Edinburgh EH2 4RG

Tel: 0131 228 8484

Email: info@childreninscotland.org.uk

Citizens Advice Scotland (www.cas.org.uk)

The Scottish Citizens Advice Bureau Service is free, independent, confidential and impartial. Citizens Advice Scotland (CAS) is the umbrella organisation for all Scottish citizens advice bureaux and can help you locate your local CAB for advice and information.

Spectrum House (1st Floor)
2 Powderhall Road
Edinburgh EH7 4GB

Tel: 0131 550 1000

Email: info@cas.org.uk

Cl@n childlaw (www.clanchildlaw.org)

cl@n childlaw is an outreach law centre providing free legal services for children and young people in Edinburgh and the Lothians. They provide representation at tribunals, such as appeals against school exclusions, additional support needs tribunals and children's hearings, and in court.

P.O. Box 23865
Edinburgh EH6 4WL

Tel: 075 275 66682

Email: info@clanchildlaw.org

Comann nam Pàrant (www.parant.org.uk)

Comann nam Pàrant (CnP), which means "Parents' Organisation", consists of a network of around 30 local groups, representing the interests of parents whose children are educated through the medium of Gaelic at the various levels, from pre-school to secondary level.

The website includes contact details for local groups.

Email: fios@parant.org.uk

Common Ground Mediation
(www.commongroundmediation.co.uk)

Common Ground Mediation provides an independent Additional Support Needs (ASN) mediation service within the Scottish education system and also offers other types of mediation.

PO Box 28094
Edinburgh EH16 6WH

Tel: 0131 664 9324 or 07760 486 465

Email: info@commongroundmediation.co.uk

Educational Maintenance Allowances Scotland
(www.emascotland.com)

EMAs provide financial support to all eligible young people from low income families who undertake a full time course at school or college. The programme is managed by your Local Education Authority or your College.

Enquire (www.enquire.org.uk)

Enquire is the Scottish advice and information service for Additional Support for Learning. It is managed by Children in Scotland and funded by the Scottish Government. The service is available to parents and carers of children and young people with additional support needs, to children and young people themselves, and to professionals working with them.

Enquire offers advice and information by way of: a telephone helpline and online enquiry service; free guides, factsheets and regular newsletters; training and talks tailored to the needs of parents and professionals; services for children including workshops and interactive pages on the website.

c/o Children in Scotland
Princes House
5 Shandwick Place
Edinburgh EH2 4RG

Helpline: 0845 123 2303

Administration: 0131 222 2425

Textphone: 0131 222 2439

Email: info@enquire.org.uk

Equality and Human Rights Commission (www.equalityhumanrights.com)

The Equality and Human Rights Commission champions equality and human rights for all, working to eliminate discrimination, reduce inequality, protect human rights and to build good relations, ensuring that everyone has a fair chance to participate in society.

Freepost RRLL-GYLB-UJTA
The Optima Building
58 Robertson Street
Glasgow G2 8DU
Tel: 0845 604 5510

Textphone: 0845 604 5520

Email: scotland@equalityhumanrights.com

European Court of Human Rights (www.echr.coe.int)

The European Court of Human Rights (ECHR) in Strasbourg was established under the European Convention on Human Rights (ECHR) of 1950. The European Convention on Human Rights, or formally named the Convention for the Protection of Human Rights and Fundamental Freedoms, is one of the most important conventions adopted by the Council of Europe. All 47 member states of the Council of Europe are signatories of the Convention. Applications against Signatory Parties can be brought before the Court either by State Parties or by individuals.

Council of Europe
F-67075 Strasbourg Cedex
France

Tel: +33 (0)3 88 41 20 18

General Teaching Council for Scotland (GTCS) (www.gtcs.org.uk)

The General Teaching Council for Scotland is the professional regulatory body for teachers in Scotland. Their responsibilities include maintaining the register of all teachers eligible to teach in public schools in Scotland, probation, continuing professional development, accrediting professional standards and assessing fitness to teach.

Clerwood House
96 Clermiston Road
Edinburgh
EH12 6UT

Tel: 0131 314 6000

Fax: 0131 314 6001

Email: gtcs@gtcs.org.uk

Govan Law Centre: Education Law Unit (www.edlaw.org.uk)

The Education Law Unit is the national expert legal resource in the field of education law, with a particular focus on legal issues affecting children or young people with additional support needs, and on equality and human rights issues at school. They provide advice, information, training, and representation services.

47 Burleigh Street
Glasgow
G51 3LB

Tel: 0141 445 1955

Email: advice@edlaw.org.uk

HM Inspectorate of Education (HMIE)
(www.scotland.gov.uk/hmie)

HMIEs' core function is to provide assurance and bring about improvement through inspection and review of all sectors of education. They work closely with partner organisations including: Scottish Government; Pre-school centres, schools, and education authorities; Parent and practitioner representative bodies; Partner inspectorates; Scottish Funding Council and Scotland's colleges; Learning and Teaching Scotland and the Scottish Qualification Authority

More information is available on their web site www.hmie.gov.uk or by contacting:

HMIE Business Management and Communications Team
Denholm House
Almondvale Business Park
Almondvale Way
Livingston
EH54 6GA

Tel: 01506 600 200

Independent Special Education Advice (Scotland)
(www.isea.org.uk)

ISEA (Scotland) provides advice, information, support, advocacy and representation services to parents who have children with additional support needs

164 High Street
Dalkeith
Midlothian
EH22 1AY

Tel: 0131 454 0144

Information Commissioners Office (www.ico.gov.uk)

The Information Commissioner's Office is the UK's independent authority set up to promote access to official information and to protect personal information.

Wycliffe House
Water Land
Wilmslow
Cheshire
SK9 5AF

Tel: 08456 306060

Lagh-Sgoile (www.lagh-sgoile.org.uk)

A gaelic language pupils' rights website designed for children and young people. The site's name, "lagh-sgoile", "school law". The website is run by Govan Law Centre.

Law Society of Scotland (www.lawscot.org.uk)

The Law Society of Scotland is the governing body for Scottish solicitors. The website has a list of accredited solicitors practicing in child law.

26 Drumsheugh Gardens
Edinburgh
EH3 7YR

Tel: 0131 226 7411

Email: lawscot@lawscot.org.uk

Learn Direct Scotland (www.learndirectscotland.com)

learndirect scotland can help you fit learning into your life. We can give you information on thousands of courses throughout Scotland and give you information funding and childcare too.

Freepost RRKE-KCTH-RASX
PO Box 26891
Glasgow
G2 9BU

Tel: 0808 1009000

Learning and Teaching Scotland (www.LTScotland.com)

Learning and Teaching Scotland, funded by the Scottish Government, is the main organisation for the development of the Scottish curriculum. A non-departmental public body, LTS is at the heart of all major developments in Scotland's education, moving forward with its partners.

The Optima
58 Robertson Street
Glasgow
G2 8DU

Customer Services Tel: 08700 100 297

Email: enquiries@LTScotland.org.uk

Contact details for all our offices are at http://www.ltscotland.org.uk/aboutlts/contact/index.asp

LGBT Youth Scotland (www.lgbtyouth.org.uk)

LGBT Youth Scotland is a national youth organisation working towards the inclusion of lesbian, gay, bisexual and transgender young people in the life of Scotland.

They provide a range of services and opportunities for young people, families and professionals in order to proactively assist with increasing awareness and confidence, in turn reducing isolation and intolerance.

You can contact LGBT Youth Scotland by calling:

Glasgow: 0141 548 8121 or 0141 552 4807

Edinburgh: 0131 622 2266

Dumfries: 01387 739888

Email: info@lgbtyouth.org.uk

Parentline Scotland (www.children1st.org.uk/parentline)

ParentLine Scotland is the free, confidential, telephone helpline for parents and anyone caring for a child in Scotland. The website has free factsheets and advice for parents. Opening times are 9am – 5pm on Monday, Wednesday and Friday, and from 9am to 9pm on Tuesday and Thursday.

c/o Children 1st
83 Whitehouse Loan
Edinburgh
EH9 1AT

Tel: 0808 800 222

Parentzone (www.parentzonescotland.gov.uk)

This site offers a broad range of information for parents, carers and others responsible for school age children. The website also provides a comprehensive list of links to useful organisations and recent publications.

Enquiries can be made via email at:
parentzone@scotland.gsi.gov.uk

Resolve ASL (www.resolveasl.org.uk)

RESOLVE:ASL Mediation Service, based within Children in Scotland, offers local authorities a fully independent means for resolving disputes with parents/carers and children and young people with additional support needs.

c/o Children in Scotland
Princes House
5 Shandwick Place
Edinburgh
EH2 4RG

Tel: 0131 222 2456

respectme (www.respectme.org.uk)

respectme, Scotland's Anti-Bullying Service, is funded by the Scottish Government and managed in partnership with SAMH (Scottish Association for Mental Health), and LGBT Youth Scotland.

respectme works with all adults who play a role in the lives of children and young people, to give them the practical skills and confidence to deal with bullying behaviour wherever it occurs. We offer free training to adults across Scotland and work with organisations at a local and strategic level to help them develop robust anti-bullying policies and practices.

Cumbrae House
15 Carlton Court
Glasgow
G5 9JP

Txt: 'respect' plus your message to 60066

Tel: 0844 800 8600

Email: enquire@respectme.org.uk

Schoolhouse Home Education Association
(www.schoolhouse.org.uk)

Schoolhouse offers information and support to parents/carers throughout Scotland who seek to take personal responsibility for the education of their children, families who have chosen, or are contemplating home-based education; and those who wish to safeguard the right of families to educate in accordance with their own philosophy and with due regard to the wishes and feelings of their children.

Schoolhouse
PO Box 18044
Glenrothes
Fife KY7 9AD

Tel: 01307 463120

Email: info@schoolhouse.org.uk

Scotland's Commissioner for Children and Young people
(www.sccyp.org.uk)

SCCYP promotes and safeguards the rights of children and young people living in Scotland. The Commissioner is here to make sure all children have their rights respected (add in) and provides a signposting and information service.

85 Holyrood Road
Edinburgh EH8 8AU

Tel: 0131 558 5480

Young Person's Freephone: 0800 019 1179

Email: inbox@sccyp.org.uk

The Anti-Bullying Network (www.antibullying.net)

A not-for-profit charity supporting pupils, teachers and parents in tackling bullying in schools and communities.

The Anti-Bullying Network
Simpson House
52 Queen Street
Edinburgh EH2 3NS

Website: www.antibullying.net

Email: info@antibullying.net

Scottish Association of Law Centres (www.salc.info)

SALC is the representative organisation for Scotland's community and user controlled law centres. All law centres are charities and aim to tackle the unmet legal needs of those in poverty and disadvantage.

Scottish Association of Law Centres (SALC)
c/o Castlemilk Law & Money Advice Centre
30-32 Dougrie Drive
Castlemilk
Glasgow G45 9AD

Tel: 0141 634 0313

Scottish Catholic Education Service (www.sces.uk.com)

The Scottish Catholic Education Service (SCES) was established by the Catholic Education Commission (CEC) on behalf of the Bishops' Conference of Scotland. While each Bishop is responsible for setting education policy to suit Diocesan needs within the local context, there are broad issues of national significance on which all the Dioceses agree general policy principles, as advised by the CEC. SCES works within the parameters of these national issues to offer support to schools, parishes and Dioceses.

75 Craigpark
Glasgow
G31 2HD

Email: mail@sces.uk.com

Scottish Child Law Centre (www.sclc.org.uk)

The Scottish Child Law Centre is a charity based in Edinburgh that serves the whole of Scotland. The Centre promotes the understanding of children's rights and how Scottish Law affects children and young people Free legal information and advice is available by contacting the Centre.

Free texts for under 18's: text SCLC and your question to 80800.

54 East Crosscauseway
Edinburgh EH8 9HD

Tel: 0131 667 6333

Email: enquiries@sclc.org.uk

Scottish Council of Independent Schools (www.scis.org.uk)

The Scottish Council of Independent Schools (SCIS) promotes and supports the significant contribution made by independent schools to education in Scotland. Within this website you will find full and comprehensive details of all independent Scottish schools represented by SCIS.

SCIS
21 Melville Street
Edinburgh EH3 7PE

Tel: 0131 220 2106

Email: information@scis.org.uk

Scottish Council for Research in Education (www.scre.ac.uk)

SCRE's functions are to conduct educational research of the highest quality and to support the use of research outcomes through the dissemination of findings.

The SCRE Centre
Faculty of Education
University of Glasgow
11 Eldon Street
Glasgow G3 6NH

Email: scre.info@scre.ac.uk

The devolved Government for Scotland is responsible for most of the issues of day-to-day concern to the people of Scotland, including health, education, justice, rural affairs, and transport.

The Government was known as the Scottish Executive when it was established in 1999 following the first elections to the Scottish Parliament. The current administration was formed after elections in May 2007.

Scottish Government
Victoria Quay
Edinburgh EH6 6QQ

Tel: 08457 741 741 or 0131 556 8400

Minicom: +44 (0)131 244 1829 (service for the deaf)

Email: ceu@scotland.gsi.gov.uk

Scottish Legal Aid Board (www.slab.org.uk)

Legal aid allows people who would not otherwise be able to afford it to get help for their legal problems. The Scottish Legal Aid Board is responsible for managing legal aid in Scotland.

44 Drumsheugh Gardens
Edinburgh EH3 7SW

Legal Aid Helpline (for members of the public seeking information about how to get legal aid): 0845 122 8686

Tel: 0131 226 7061

Email: general@slab.org.uk

Scottish Muslim Parents Association (www.smpa.org.uk)

The purpose of SMPA shall be to provide better understanding to parents of the policies of Scottish Government's Departments including education and training, health and community care.

113 Commerce Street
Glasgow G5 8DL

Tel: 07941305074

Email: smpa_info@smpa.org.uk

Scottish Parent Teacher Council (www.sptc.info)

The SPTC aims to advance education by encouraging the fullest co-operation between home and school, education authorities, central government and all those concerned with education in Scotland. It is a national membership body for parents' groups in schools.

53 George Street
Edinburgh EH2 2HT

Tel / Fax: 0131 226 4378

Email: sptc@sptc.info

Scottish Parent Council Association (www.scottishparents.com)

The Scottish Parent Councils Association, a reconstituted body founded in 1991, represents the interests of Parent Councils across Scotland following the abolition of Schools Boards and the introduction of Parent Councils

Newall Terrace
Dumfries DG1 1LW

Tel: 01387 260 428

Email: info@scottishparents.com

Scottish Parliament (www.scottish.parliament.uk)

The Scottish Parliament is the law-making body for devolved matters in Scotland

Edinburgh EH99 1SP

Tel: 0800 092 7500

Email: sp.info@scottish.parliament.uk

Scottish Public Services Ombudsman (www.spso.org.uk)

The SPSO is the final stage for complaints about organisations providing public services in Scotland. They deal with complaints about councils, the National Health Service, housing associations, the Scottish Government and its agencies and departments, colleges and universities and most Scottish public bodies. The service is independent, impartial and free.

4 Melville Street
Edinburgh EH3 7NS

Tel: 0800 377 7330

Text: 0790 049 4372

Email: ask@spso.org.uk

Scottish Qualifications Authority (www.sqa.org.uk)

The SQA is the national body in Scotland responsible for the development, accreditation, assessment and certification of qualifications other than degrees. The overall aim of the SQA is to manage the qualifications system below degree level to allow students to fulfil their potential to participate in the economy, society and communities of Scotland.

The Optima Building
58 Robertson Street
Glasgow G2 8DQ

Tel: 0845 279 1000

Email: customer@sqa.org.uk

**Scottish Throughcare and Aftercare Forum
(www.scottishthroughcare.org.uk)**

The Scottish Throughcare & Aftercare Forum is a voluntary organisation whose aim is to improve support for young people leaving residential or foster care in Scotland.

37 Otago Street (2nd Floor)
Glasgow G12 8JJ

Tel: 0141 357 4124

Email: enquiries@scottishthroughcare.org.uk

Skill Scotland (www.skill.org.uk)

Skill is a national charity promoting opportunities for young people and adults with any kind of disability, impairment or long-term health condition in post-16 education, training and employment across the UK.

Norton Park
57 Albion Road
Edinburgh EH7 5QY

Tel: 0131 475 2348

Email: admin@skillscotland.org.uk

Student Loans Company (www.slc.co.uk)

The Student Loans Company is a not-for-profit organisation providing loans and grants to people in Higher Education. We are owned by the Department for Innovation, Universities & Skills and Scottish ministers. We were set up in 1989 as a limited company. We work with HM Revenue & Customs in managing repayment of student loans, and we also collect direct debit repayments on loans issued before 1998.

100 Bothwell Street
Glasgow G2 7JD

Tel: 0845 026 2109

Universities and Colleges Admission Services (UCAS) (www.ucas.com)

UCAS is the central organisation that processes applications for full-time undergraduate courses at UK universities and colleges

Rosehill
New Barn Lane
Cheltenham GL52 3LZ

Tel: 01242 222444